The Bear Goes South

When Russia Invades Israel

By David Egner

CONTENTS

PREFACE

This book is about the coming invasion of Israel by Russia. World conditions show that it may be impending—or even imminent. Therefore, I believe the only passage of the Bible where this event is prophesied, Ezekiel 38 and 39, needs close examination by every student of the Scriptures.

I suggest that you read these chapters carefully. They speak of a serious confrontation between two representatives of an all-important institution raised up by God—the nations. Consequently, a look at God's purpose for the nations and their destiny is an important part of this study of the coming Russo-Israeli war.

The book is written in a modern context. The people who come down from "the north parts" could only be living in Russia. Whether or not they will be ruled by the Communists when the events described by Ezekiel come to pass cannot be determined with certainty. Another thousand years could pass before the invasion takes place, but I really don't think so. That's why I have written the book as if the northern invaders are motivated by Communist ideologies.

David Egner

INTRODUCTION: The Rise of Nations

For all of its drawbacks, the Middle Ages was not a bad time to be alive. Life was uncomplicated for the average man. He tilled his meager acreage. He paid taxes to his feudal lord. And he fought his wars for him (usually with a cantankerous neighboring lord). In return he accepted protection and justice from his master. He worshiped regularly, he said his morning and evening prayers, and he gave liberally to the church from his meager income. To please the Heavenly Lord, he even worked at night to help build the town's cathedral. His hopes and dreams were in the next world, not in this. Faith was superior to reason in medieval times.

But the curtain that closed the Middle Ages reopened to a whole new way of life for man. The Renaissance brought drastic changes. New lands were explored and new products made available. Philosophers and theologians rediscovered the beauties and delights of this present world and felt free to enjoy them. Money came into circulation. Vassals were able to buy their land from their lords. The crusades revealed the inadequacies of the medieval system. Invention, exploration, discovery—these made life much more complex for the common man. Slowly, ever so slowly, the church gave ground to a new force in Western Europe—the nation. In man's thinking, faith and reason became equal.

Then came the Enlightenment, when reason was made superior to faith. The French humanist Voltaire wrote, "What a light has burst across Europe within the past few years! It first illuminated all the princes of the North; it has even come into the universities. It is the light of common sense" (*Last Remarks on the 'Pensees' of Pascal*). The groundswell of placing hope in man's intellect became a tidal wave; reason was almost deified. Men decided they would use their intelligence to control their environment; they didn't need God anymore.

Tragically, the organized church agreed. As has so often happened in history, the established clergy saw which way the trend was going and went along with it. The English deists decided that God had indeed left mankind to manage his own affairs with the best use of his reason. God was the great clockmaker: man was to keep it running. Alexander Pope expressed it in *Essay on Man* when he said that reason is man's greatest gift. Along with this thinking came a surge of unbridled optimism. People really felt they could solve every human problem, and that a perfect world lay just around the corner.

In conjunction with this mood of self-confidence came the rise of nationalism. The state would take the place of God, doing for mankind what the church had tried to do and failed. Walt Whitman expressed the thinking of the world in his *Song to America,* when he wrote, "Come, I will make thee a continent indissoluble; I will make the most splendid race the sun ever shone upon." The "I" in this line is not God; it's the nation.

For a while, history seemed to be cooperating. The 18th century went on without a major war. Great strides forward were made during the industrial revolution. Communication, transportation, and commerce grew immensely. Amazing inventions made life better and easier. Everyone was prospering. August Comte spoke of a new "religion of humanity," and Charles Darwin's *Origin of the Species* implied that man, the apex of the evolutionary process, was about to reach his highest plane. The nations were bringing in utopia; reason was the key to man's glorious future.

But murmurs of doubt began to be heard. Some foresaw the horrors of domination by the state. Others feared ambitious dictators, and still others were sensitive to the inequities of modern life. A German philosopher, Karl Marx, looked for a way to correct the imbalances. His solution was dialectical materialism, or, as it is better known today, communism.

The world erupted like a fiery volcano in the 20th century. A deep recession was followed by World War I. Millions died or were left homeless because of the armed aggression of ambitious nations. Then came the Great Depression of the 1930s, followed instantly by another world war—even more terrible than the first. As it ended, the rumble of 1,000-pound bombs was swallowed up by the deafening blasts of two atomic explosions. Pessimism pervaded art, literature, and philosophy. Mankind became smaller, of less worth, and more afraid. Reason was creating megalomaniacs, monsters who were unsated by power and cruel in their oppression. Individuality had shrunken and lost all meaning. The state had almost forgotten that ordinary men existed.

Nationalism has reached its ugliest epitome, many feel, in the Union of Socialist Soviet Republics. The quest for power and world supremacy, the thirst for worldwide "clout" at conference tables and in economic centers, and the drive to spread the sphere of national domination to its widest possible perimeters have been most clearly demonstrated in the past 40 years by the Soviet Union. The brutality of a single dictator—Joseph Stalin—sent millions of his own countrymen to their deaths. The people of Eastern Europe, so often victimized over the centuries, were swallowed up as satellites by a policy of inhuman terrorism. In time, China fell to communist dictators. Cuba came into the fold of Russian influence. Mongolia is all but annexed. Iran totters on the brink of Soviet domination. Afghanistan has virtually capitulated to the Soviets. Chile has felt Russia's force, as have several of her South American neighbors. Italy and France are in deep jeopardy. Vietnam is gone, as is Cambodia. This creeping tide of aggression and domination by force—nationalism at its worst—is most fearsome. By all appearances, the Russian Communists will not stop until they have the world by the throat, or are themselves beaten down in defeat.

Why did God allow nations to rise up anyway? Didn't He know it would come to this? What does the Bible say about the countries of the world? Will Russia succeed? Is Israel in danger of Soviet invasion? This book has been written to answer these vital questions from God's Word. As you read it, please thank God for the freedom that is yours—and for the hope of Christ's soon coming to make all things just and right.

1
The Nations in God's Plan

"I will set My glory among the nations . . ."

One of the most astounding occurrences of recent history has been the emergence of Russia as a world power. Less than five decades ago she was still locked in the dark ages, a lethargic giant lulled into slumber by centuries of poverty, exploitation, ruthless domination, and contrary natural conditions.

But the introduction of communist ideology, along with the united, heroic effort to withstand Nazi invasion, has prodded the great Russian bear to wakefulness. She has yawned, stretched, and blinked her eyes at the modern world. Slowly, steadily, irrepressively, she has flexed her muscles and begun to move. The statements by the prophet Ezekiel that depict her as a mighty military force—statements that seemed an absurdity only a few years ago—have become a frightening reality. The prospect of the bear going south, of Russia invading Israel, has become a very real possibility. Students of prophecy are no longer saying "if" but "when."

But before we can understand just where Russia fits into Bible prophecy, we must begin with a study of the nations in world history and in God's program. As we learn how they began, discern what their purpose is, consider their relation to Israel, and study what their future will be, we will be able to put the events of the Middle East and Russia in scriptural perspective. In this chapter, after tracing the origin of nations, we will look at Daniel's outline of world history. Then we'll draw some conclusions about the role of the nations in God's plan for Israel and all mankind.

THE BEGINNING OF NATIONS

The opening chapters of Genesis tell of man's creation and the entrance of sin into the world. In the garden of Eden our first parents fellowshiped openly with God and answered directly to Him. Then Adam's choice to disobey the Lord led to his expulsion from the garden, and thus began a steady course of moral degeneration. It reached its lowest limits in Noah's day, when the entire race was given over to unbelievable cruelty and wickedness. The Bible described it as follows:

> And God saw that the wickedness of man was great in the earth, and that every imagination of the thoughts of his heart was only evil continually.

> And it repented the Lord that He had made man on the earth, and it grieved Him at His heart.
>
> And the Lord said, I will destroy man whom I have created from the face of the earth; both man, and beast, and the creeping thing, and the fowls of the air; for it repenteth Me that I have made them (Genesis 6:5-7).

Only Noah remained true to God. We are told that he alone "found grace in the eyes of the Lord" (Genesis 6:8). So God destroyed the race in a great flood—all except Noah, his three sons, and their wives.

When the flood waters receded and Noah and his family left the ark, mankind had a new beginning. For the first time God gave men the responsibility of governing themselves. Adam had been told to subdue the earth, but he had fallen short of satisfying the Lord. Now this same command was reinstated, and a new obligation was added. God commanded, "Whoso sheddeth man's blood, by man shall his blood be shed; for in the image of God made He man" (Genesis 9:6).

The principle of human government, enacted by these words, has never been rescinded. The sword of human justice is in man's own hand. He is to judge and punish the wanton lawlessness of a fallen, sinful humanity. This ancient principle is restated and clarified in Romans 13:1-7. In this key New Testament passage, mankind is told to be subject to governmental leaders because they are "ordained of God" (v. 1). So closely are these national rulers identified with the Lord that the person who resists them "resisteth the ordinance of God; and they that resist shall receive to themselves judgment"

(v. 2). In fact, the ruler is called a "minister of God, an avenger to execute wrath" (v. 4). The main function of the nations, therefore, is to give man a means of governing himself. He had already shown in the days from Adam to Noah that he could not do so individually.

Sadly, in the course of history, human government has failed. Tyranny, injustice, and cruelty have caused millions to live in poverty and unhappiness. As with Adam and with individuals, the nations have rebelled against the Lord. They have failed in the divine purpose for which they were established.

PROPHECY ABOUT NOAH'S SONS

The Lord did not leave men to grope in darkness, but used the events of Noah's day to mark out the path of the future. For example, God promised never again to destroy the race by water, and gave the rainbow as a sign of His covenant (Genesis 9:13-17).

Specific prophecies about the nations were also given. They came as the consequence of a dismal day in Noah's life. The patriarch had planted vineyards when he left the ark. Later he became drunk on the wine and lay naked in his tent. Shem and Japheth respected their father and covered him; Ham did not. God pronounced His will for the sins of Noah and the nations that would rise from them in these words:

> And he said, Cursed be Canaan; a servant of servants shall he be unto his brethren.
>
> And he said, Blessed be the Lord God of Shem; and Canaan shall be his servant.
>
> God shall enlarge Japheth, and he shall dwell in the tents of Shem; and Canaan shall be his servant (Genesis 9:25-27).

According to this prophecy, all of mankind would be divided according to Noah's sons. The descendants of Canaan, youngest son of Ham (who perhaps was with him when he discovered Noah), would be a servant people. Shem, however, would be Ham's master, and would experience God's blessing. Israel was descended from Shem. And Japheth was promised "enlargement." As progenitor of the Western European nations, he would control vast land areas and contribute significantly to human progress. The Russian people are descendants of Japheth.

IMPORTANCE OF GENESIS 10

The chapter following the judgment upon Noah's sons is often overlooked in Bible study, yet it is one of the most important in the entire Old Testament. As one studies it carefully, he finds the background for the nations as they gradually took form in the centuries following Noah's emergence from the ark. They are divided according to his three sons as prophesied. They are still identifiable today, even though they commingled and intermarried throughout the centuries.

From a biblical perspective, the sons of Shem (the Semites) were the most important. The Assyrians, Syrians, Arabian peoples, Chaldeans, and Israelites were all in the line of Shem. Through Abraham, progenitor of the Jews, the revelation of God and fulfillment of His redemptive plan were given to the human race.

The descendants of Ham occupied much of the Middle East region. The Canaanites, of course, are one of the more familiar ethnic groups to Bible students. So are the

Egyptians, the Phoenicians, the Hittites, and the Babylonians. The nations of the Orient also very likely descended from Ham.

But we are especially interested in our study in the offspring of Japheth, the one whose tent God said would be "enlarged." He would prosper, and would govern many peoples. Anthropologists are generally agreed that Japheth's offspring settled north and west of Israel from the Arctic Circle to Spain and the British Isles. The descendants of Gomer, son of Japheth, settled in the far North. Some inhabited western Russia, the region north of the Black Sea, and Armenia. Magog, also a son of Japheth, was forerunner of the Scythians, who settled in central Russia. Other sons were progenitors of the Greeks, the Medes, the Trojans, the Dalmatians (who inhabited southeastern Europe), and the residents of Spain and Western Europe.

The Russians came originally from Japheth's line. So also did all of the important people of Western Europe. Japheth's sons, in actuality, formulated the bulk of the major Gentile nations. They have the lead in the development of western civilization, and they will play a major role in the prophetic end-time events.

DANIEL'S OUTLINE OF HISTORY

The study of the nations and their development is made more clear by a look at the prophecies of Daniel. This faithful prophet, exiled along with many of his countrymen in Babylon, was the means God used to reveal in broad outline the major peoples and significant events of world history.

The first prophetic foreview did not come

to Daniel, but to Nebuchadnezzar, king of Babylon. This oriental despot had been searching for information about the future, wondering "what should come to pass hereafter" (Daniel 2:29). God told him in a dream, but in the morning he couldn't remember what he had envisioned. Sensing the dream's importance, he sought someone who could tell it to him and interpret it. When no one could, all the wise men were sentenced to be executed. Daniel, along with the three Hebrew young men who would later be thrown into the fiery furnace, earnestly prayed to the Lord. God gave Daniel the dream and its interpretation. When he stood before the king, he said,

> Thou, O king, sawest, and behold a great image. This great image, whose brightness was excellent, stood before thee, and the form of it was terrible.
>
> This image's head was of fine gold, its breast and its arms of silver, its belly and its thighs of bronze.
>
> Its legs of iron, its feet part of iron and part of clay,
>
> Thou sawest until a stone was cut out without hands, which smote the image upon its feet that were of iron and clay, and broke them to pieces.
>
> Then were the iron, the clay, the bronze, the silver, and the gold, broken to pieces together, and became like the chaff of the summer threshing floors; and the wind carried them away, that no place was found for them; and the stone that smote the image became a great mountain, and filled the whole earth (Daniel 2:31-35).

Daniel then went on to interpret what he had seen. Four great empires would follow one another across the stage of world history, each represented by a different segment of the idol. The head of gold was Nebuchadnezzar himself, king of the Babylonians and by far the most esteemed ruler of his day. The second kingdom, the shoulders of silver, was the Medo-Persian Empire. The third, the torso of bronze, was ancient Greece. The fourth, legs and feet of iron and iron mixed with clay, was mighty Rome. In succession, these great world powers ruled large portions of the earth's land area and human population. The diminishing of the value of the metals in the dream pictured their decreasing moral and spiritual qualities.

DANIEL'S DREAM

The second glimpse of the future nations of the world came to Daniel many years later in a vision. It is described in the opening verses of Daniel 7.

> In the first year of Belshazzar, king of Babylon, Daniel had a dream and visions of his head upon his bed; then he wrote the dream, and told the sum of the matters.
>
> Daniel spoke and said, I saw in my vision by night, and, behold, the four winds of the heaven strove upon the great sea.
>
> And four great beasts came up from the sea, diverse one from another.
>
> The first was like a lion, and had eagle's wings; I beheld till its wings were plucked, and it was lifted up from the earth, and made stand upon the feet as a man; and a man's heart was given to it.
>
> And, behold, another beast, a second, like a bear, and it raised up itself on one side, and it had three ribs in the mouth of it between its teeth; and they said thus unto it, Arise, devour much flesh.
>
> After this I beheld, and, lo, another, like a

> leopard, which had upon its back four wings of a fowl; the beast had also four heads, and dominion was given to it.
>
> After this I saw in the night visions, and, behold, a fourth beast, dreadful and terrible, and strong exceedingly, and it had great iron teeth; it devoured and broke in pieces, and stamped the residue with its feet; and it was diverse from all the beasts that were before it, and it had ten horns (Daniel 7:1-7).

Once again the four great world powers were represented, but Daniel saw them in a different light. Nebuchadnezzar had seen their glory, as represented in the metals of the image. The prophet, however, saw their true nature—beastlike creatures of enormous strength, hungry for prominence, wealth, and power. Babylon was represented by a lion, Medo-Persia as a lopsided bear, Greece as a winged leopard, and Rome as a terrible beast with great iron teeth and 10 horns. Again a degeneration in moral quality is clearly represented.

A word should be said about the fourth kingdom, represented in the statue by legs and feet of iron and clay, and in the vision as a fierce beast with 10 horns. Not all of the prophecies about this kingdom, interpreted by virtually every Bible scholar as Rome, have been fulfilled. Someday in the future, therefore, this kingdom will be revived, achieve great prominence, and play a key role in the unfolding of the endtime events. Its return as a world power will have a great bearing upon both Russia and Israel, as we shall see in later chapters.

THE PURPOSE FOR THE NATIONS

In this chapter we have discussed the beginning of the nations and traced the course of their prophetic development. After the fall, the descendants of Adam were expected to govern themselves on an individual basis. Apparently every man was to be personally responsible to the Lord, just as Adam had been in Eden. But the system did not work because of man's sinfulness. He fell further and further into disobedience and wickedness until God destroyed all but Noah and his family in the great flood.

Thus the race began anew, with Noah's three sons forming the major divisions of mankind. From them developed the nations of the world. These nations were raised up by the Lord to fulfill three important functions:

First, the nations were given the *responsibility for human government.* Man had proved that he could not individually rule himself; therefore, governors were appointed in the form of leaders of the nations. Control, order, and law were to be given the people by their governmental authorities, who were granted their power by God Himself and were to be viewed as His representatives.

But once again man failed. The rulers were no more successful at bringing justice, peace, and righteousness than were individuals. As successive world powers came and went, they were more and more degenerate. Brutality and wickedness were increasingly prevalent. God and His program were entirely left out of the picture. And the worst of the lot, the Roman Empire, will one day be revived. This time it will be even more deceitful and evil than ever before.

Second, the nations were placed in the world *to work God's will with Israel.* She was to be a witness to them; they would both bring her harassment and provide her a haven. Egypt rescued her from starvation in Jacob's day, and was a place of refuge for the infant Messiah. The United States today is Israel's friend, as was Great Britain during and after the second World War. But most of the nations have despised the Jews. Some, such as Babylon, Assyria, and Rome, have been used to judge and punish her. Even today, enemies virtually surround Israel. Though living among many peoples in this dispensation, she has seldom been welcomed, and more often been despised, persecuted, and cruelly mistreated.

Third, the nations were ordained by the Lord, along with their rulers, *to bring glory to God.* If they would bring peace and justice to the world, the Lord would be magnified, and His name made known throughout the earth. Seldom in history has this been the case. As the centuries have passed, just the opposite has been true. Disobedience has been the rule. God's chosen nation Israel has suffered at the hands of ruthless Gentile powers. Russia, the great bear to the North, has epitomized the selfish ambitions and shameful disgraces of the nations. Yet the prophets have foreseen another chapter in her dealings with God and His people. That's what the remainder of this book is all about.

2
Israel among the Nations

"... gathered out of many peoples"

Of necessity, the Israelis are brutally realistic about their relationship with the Soviet Union. They know full well that they are the major roadblock to Russian domination in the Middle East. Their soldiers have been killed by bullets fired from Russian-made rifles. Their tanks have been blown to pieces by Soviet-built "sagger" rockets. Israel's bitterest enemies have been armed with weapons from the powerful, efficient arsenals of the U.S.S.R., and the Jews have counted their dead because of it. During the 1973 war, Defense Minister Moshe Dayan said flatly, "We are at war with Russia!"

It's only natural that Israel, the chosen people of God, should come into conflict with the humanistic, "superman" thinking of Soviet communism. Though disobedient, the Jews are still God's special people. In the eyes of the world they stand for what He represents—holiness, justice, and freedom. For this reason alone they are hated.

In addition, their strong pro-Western sympathies and backing from the United States make them a powerful force for independence and democracy in the Middle East. They're tough and they're determined. When the Russian bear looks *south,* all he sees is Israel—a stubborn roadblock to Soviet expansion. With Iran becoming militantly Islamic and Egypt now looking toward the West, the bear may be getting impatient. The time could be approaching when he'll begin to move.

Israel has always played a disruptive role among the nations. She has been described by one of her own writers as "a thorn in the side of the world." The roots of these bitter feelings began in ancient history. In this chapter we will examine Israel's favored position in God's program, her troubled past, her current role in world affairs, and her tumultuous future among the nations as set forth by the prophets. As we do, the relationship between Israel and the Soviet Union will become more clear. And the stage will be set for a serious discussion of the coming Russian invasion of Israel.

ISRAEL'S UNIQUE HISTORY

The nation of Israel actually came into being when God called Abraham, descendant of Shem through Eber, to become the progenitor of a special nation. He singled him out from among the Chaldeans, instructed him to leave his homeland for an unspecified destination, and gave special promises to him and his offspring. The Bible records the covenant between God and Abraham as follows:

> Now the Lord had said unto Abram, Get thee out of thy country, and from thy kindred, and from thy father's house, unto a land that I will show thee;
>
> And I will make of thee a great nation, and I will bless thee, and make thy name great; and thou shalt be a blessing.
>
> And I will bless them that bless thee, and curse him that curseth thee: and in thee shall all families of the earth be blessed (Genesis 12:1-3).

Five times the Lord appeared to Abraham to repeat or add to the covenant He had made. A summary of the promises that formulate the basis of that covenant gives an indication of the unusual position Abraham's descendants, the Israelites, would have among the nations of the world. The following specifics are relevant:

1. Abraham would have a great name, and would receive the Lord's personal blessing (Genesis 12:2).
2. All who blessed Abraham would be blessed; all who cursed him would be cursed (Genesis 12:3).
3. All the nations of the earth would be blessed through his seed (Genesis 12:3; 22:18).
4. Abraham's offspring would multiply to become a numerous people (Genesis 13:16; 15:5).
5. Abraham and his descendants were promised the land of Palestine, forever, from "the river of Egypt" to the Euphrates (Genesis 12:7; 15:18-21).

6. Abraham's seed would conquer their enemies from among the nations: ". . . thy seed shall possess the gate of his enemies" (Genesis 22:17).
7. The covenant promises were everlasting (Genesis 17:19).
8. Kings would come from Abraham's line (Genesis 17:6).

These promises are the foundation for understanding Israel's unique role among the nations of the world. She is God's favored people. Those who bless her will benefit; those who oppose her will suffer. Palestine was deeded to her by God forever.

Additional revelation came to David, beloved by God and Israel's greatest king. He was anointed as Israel's ruler while Saul was still on the throne, though he did not ascend to power for several years. The nation prospered and expanded when he finally received the crown. He saw Israel become the most prominent nation of the Middle East. But David was dismayed that God "dwelt" only in a tent while he himself lived in a palace. So he decided to build Him a house of cedar. But Nathan the prophet denied his request and delivered to him these words from the Lord:

> And when thy days be fulfilled, and thou shalt sleep with thy fathers, I will set up thy seed after thee, which shall proceed out of thine own body, and I will establish his kingdom.
>
> He shall build an house for My name, and I will establish the throne of his kingdom forever.
>
> I will be his father, and he shall be My son. If he commit iniquity, I will chasten

> him with the rod of men, and with the stripes of the children of men;
>
> But My mercy shall not depart away from him, as I took it from Saul, whom I put away before thee.
>
> And thine house and thy kingdom shall be established forever before thee; thy throne shall be established forever (2 Samuel 7:12-16).

An analysis of this text shows that David was promised a son who would build the temple, that David's throne would continue forever, and that his kingdom would be everlasting. The covenant was repeated several times in the Old Testament (Isaiah 9:6; Jeremiah 23:5,6) and confirmed in the New (Luke 1:30-33; Acts 15:14-18). Although the throne has been empty for many years, as prophesied in Hosea 3:4,5, the promise of God remains in effect. Israel still exists as a nation. The day is coming when a descendant of David will once again reign in Jerusalem. Therefore, on the national and international scene, Israel is a force to be reckoned with. And no one knows it better than the Arab nations and Russia.

ISRAEL'S UNIQUE CALLING

Israel is indeed God's chosen people. She has been singled out to receive special blessings and has been granted numerous promises. The Jews are linked by divine mandate to the land of Israel. But they have also been called to fulfill a unique purpose among the people of the world.

A Commissioned People. When the Lord singled out Abraham, He was in effect narrowing down His redemptive activity to one nation, though all the world would benefit.

He had promised Abraham that. But the Lord would work His plan of salvation for all mankind through the descendants of this special individual. When Adam sinned, God did not turn His back upon the human race. Rather, He put into motion a plan that had been formulated "before the foundations of the world." He would use the nation of Israel to teach mankind about His holiness and the awfulness of sin. He would establish the sacrificial system as a means of illustrating the method of redemption. And he would single out first Abraham, then Isaac, then Jacob, then Judah and his seed, then David to be the fathers of the line through which He would send the Last Adam into the world. That One, Jesus of Nazareth, would perfectly obey the law, would suffer and die as our substitute, and would be raised again to show that God's holy demands had been fully satisfied. Salvation would then be proclaimed to the whole world. Yes, redemption would come to mankind through Israel, the chosen nation of God.

Second, Israel would be the vehicle of God's revelation. Through her writers—poets, prophets, historians, and philosophers—He would make His mind known to men. These inspired authors would record the unfolding drama of redemption. Men from among the Jews would write down salvation's story—from its beginnings in Eden through mighty events like the crossing of the Red Sea, the receiving of the law, the conquest of Canaan, the monarchy, and on into New Testament days—these men would record, under the direction of the Holy Spirit, the significant events of salvation's story. Poets would express their worship and praise to God. Select men would be given glimpses of the future and would write down what they foresaw for all to read. Yes, God would use Israel to tell the story of His ways with mankind.

Third, Israel was to be a witness to the nations. Her worship of one God, her stringent moral code, and her sacrificial system spoke to the world of a living God who had revealed Himself. Her prophets would point accusing fingers at the idolatrous practices of her pagan neighbors, condemning their immorality. As her people obeyed the Lord, offered Him true worship through sacrifices and obedience, and cleansed their hearts from sin, they would be proclaiming the mercy and goodness of God to all the nations.

Fourth, the Savior of mankind would come through the Jews. When the time had come, the One so long promised was born into the world in Bethlehem of a Jewish virgin named Mary. He was called Jesus. When He began His public ministry, He taught great things and authenticated His claims by working miracles. Then He was rejected by His countrymen and crucified. But "this same Jesus," resurrected and ascended to the Father, will one day return as King of kings and Lord of lords. The Jews will acknowledge Him as the true Messiah and turn to Him in faith. And in Him, through faith, all the nations of earth will experience untold blessing.

A Chastised Nation. The expectations were high for Israel as they came out of Egypt. If they walked with God and obeyed His laws, they would experience peace and prosperity. But Israel failed. Time after time her people rebelled against the Lord and went their own way. In the wilderness they refused to listen to the minority report of the two spies who said Canaan could be conquered. As a result, they failed to take possession of the land God had promised them. Then, after 40 years of desert wandering until a whole new generation had taken control, they crossed the Jordan and enjoyed one victory after another. Though God had told them to occupy *all* the land, they did not; tiring of battle and weakening in faith, they were content to capture only the central highlands.

Later they demanded a king, in spite of God's clear warnings through Moses that it would lead to trouble. After the glory years of David and Solomon, they again turned their backs upon the Lord. Solomon allowed his pagan wives to worship their false deities, and the gods of the surrounding nations were introduced to the populace. After King Solomon died, the kingdom was divided. Heathen deities were worshiped in groves and high places throughout Israel. God grew tired of the adulterous hearts of His people. First Israel, then Judah, fell captive to foreign domination.

The Jews' greatest act of disobedience and rejection occurred some five centuries after Malachi wrote the last book of the Old Testament. Jesus Christ was born in exact fulfillment of the Hebrew prophecies. He lived a sinless life. He taught the people of Israel that He was the Son of God. He proved it by doing only those things that God can rightfully do—raising the dead, forgiving sin, controlling nature, and receiving worship. But Israel's leaders hated Him. He did not fit their preconceived idea of the Messiah, and He refused to condone their self-righteous, deceitful practices. They soon succeeded in turning the masses against Him. They bullied Pilate into permitting Him to be executed on a Roman cross.

Think of it! The King of Glory walked among men. He resisted all sin. He taught the very truths of God. His every act was loving, merciful, compassionate, and Spirit-directed. Yet His own people rejected Him. He fulfilled every prophetic detail about the Messiah during His lifetime. Yet the Jews unwittingly carried out the predictions of Scripture when they crucified Him. The self-righteous, wicked Israelites would not be satisfied until He lay dead at their feet.

And so God sent retribution once again. The Roman army closed in, and hundreds of thousands of Jews died. The rest were exiled from their beloved Palestine in A.D. 130, scattered to the four corners of the earth. They would remain in exile for some 1800 years, dispersed among hostile people and living far away from the beloved rolling hills and fertile plains of the land of promise.

ISRAEL'S PRESENT CONDITION

But the world has witnessed an amazing miracle in the past few decades. Israel has come back to the land! A century ago, only about 10,000 Jews lived in Palestine; today there are nearly 4 million. Until World War II, their homeland was in the hands of the Turks; now Palestine has been recognized as an independent Jewish state and has successfully fought three major wars.

It hasn't been easy for the Jews. The movement to return began in the late 19th century. Here and there groups of Jews sought to buy land in Palestine and began to settle.

The Arabs would only sell them the worst of locations with terrible soil conditions. Nevertheless, they came—and they stayed.

Then a highly educated Budapest Jew named Theodore Herzl began to proclaim the doctrines of Zionism. "We are a people—one people," he claimed, and in 1896 he published a powerful piece of literature called *Der Judenstaat*, "The Jew-state." Herzl saw only one clear pathway ahead for the Jews of the world—a global regathering of Israelites to a land of their own.

The movement caught hold and began to grow. With financial backing from many quarters, hundreds of acres of land were purchased in Palestine, and the Jews began to return in large numbers.

Two significant events occurred in 1917 to help the Zionist cause. The first was the Balfour Declaration, which called for a "national home" for the Jews. This meant the establishment of a "Jewish State" in the promised land, and the Jews were ecstatic. British policy now supported a home in Palestine for Israel! A second important event in 1917 was British General Allenby's capture of Jerusalem. Jewish youths enthusiastically joined his forces and fought valiantly against the Turks. The fact that Israeli soldiers were fighting on Palestinian soil helped fan the flames of Jewish nationalism around the world.

Jewish independence was finally realized in 1948. But the moment her Declaration of Independence was declared, the Arabs attacked! In the bitter fighting that followed, the Jews fought courageously and successfully. Finally peace was declared, and Israel was in Palestine to stay. After nearly 19 centuries of wandering and exile, a sovereign Jewish state existed in the promised land once again. Wars were fought on two and three fronts in 1967 and again in 1973. But the Jews have prevailed, and are walking today on their ancient soil—a miracle of unsurpassed proportions in the history of mankind.

Significance of Israel's Return. The fact that the Jews occupy the promised land once again has immense significance in both modern and prophetic history. For one thing, the surrounding nations are deeply disturbed. Israel's ancient enemies have not lost their hatred; if anything, it has intensified.

For another, the stage is now set for the fulfillment of the prophetic statements about the endtimes. For the final events to take place as foretold by the prophets, Israel had to be in the land. Until a few short years ago, unbelievers scoffed at biblical descriptions of a coming treaty between Israel and the ruler of the revived Roman Empire, a third temple in Jerusalem, Israelites fleeing to the mountains of Judea, and a Russian invasion of an Israeli-occupied Palestine. But not anymore, for the Jews are back!

WHAT'S AHEAD FOR ISRAEL?

After the rejection and crucifixion of Jesus Christ, God directed His attention to the Gentiles. The church was formed at Pentecost, and the gospel was preached to all. Many people from all over the world heard the message of salvation and believed. The church multiplied. Today, Christianity is one of the most powerful forces on the earth, claiming followers from every race and social station in life.

Meanwhile, through the long centuries, the Jews have had to struggle to survive. They've suffered immeasurably. But God did not turn His back on them forever. The promise to David and the prophets of a glorious kingdom has not been rescinded. In recent events of history, it seems the Lord is showing that His attention is about to be focused on Israel once again.

The regathering of the Jews to Palestine is the most clear indication. The prophets had stated clearly that God would judge Israel by scattering the people among the nations (Deuteronomy 28:63-66; Zechariah 7:13,14). But their prophets had proclaimed again and again that the people of Israel would be regathered and returned to Palestine (see Deuteronomy 30:1-3; Isaiah 11:11,12; 43:5-7; Jeremiah 16:4-15; Ezekiel 37:21,22; Hosea 3:5; Amos 9:14,15; Zechariah 8:7,8). That event is now occurring.

These same prophets also linked Israel's regathering with the endtime events. Though we cannot say with certainty that the current return of the Jews to Palestine is the fulfillment of these prophecies, all signs appear to be pointing forward to these events transpiring in the near future.

1. *The Rapture of the Church.* The next event on God's prophetic timetable is the translation of the church. At a shout from Heaven and the sound of a trumpet, Jesus Christ will take His own up to meet Him in the air. First the bodies of believers who have died will be resurrected to unite with their souls, which have been with Jesus. Then all Christians who are living will rise to join them in the clouds (see 1 Thessalonians 4:13-18; 1 Corinthians 15:51-54). Then, as Paul wrote,

we shall "ever be with the Lord" (1 Thessalonians 4:17).

2. *The Tribulation.* Once the church has been removed, the world will enter a 7-year period called the tribulation. It is during these years that Israel will endure her most dreadful persecutions. This is the time of the coming Russian invasion of Israel.

Two great purposes will be realized during these terrible days of the outpouring of God's wrath upon the earth. First, the rebellious nations will be punished for their repeated failure to fulfill the purposes for which God ordained them. Rather than bringing order, righteousness, and justice to mankind as the Lord intended, they have tolerated and sometimes fostered cruel oppression, unlawful domination, and a proud mockery of the principles of God. In the dreaded years of the tribulation, the nations will stagger helplessly under the repeated blows of divine chastisement.

Second, these very nations will be used of God to bring Israel to repentance. Antichrist, head of the revived Roman Empire, will gradually control the minds and lives of huge numbers of people. His hatred of God will be focused upon the Jews, and he will persecute them mercilessly. As his obsession with destroying Israel intensifies, he will march his armies into Palestine. Then, when things look the blackest, God will intervene. Jesus Christ will return to earth as Captain of the host of God, and Antichrist and his cohorts will be defeated in the terrible battle of Armageddon. Israel will see Christ as their political and personal Savior, and they will repent and believe. Satan's henchmen will be cast into the lake of fire, and he himself will be bound for 1,000 years. The day of Israel's glory will finally have dawned.

3. *The Millennial Kingdom.* Once He is established in Zion, Jesus Christ will initiate the long-promised kingdom of Bible prophecy. He will rule the world in righteousness, justice, and peace. Israel will be the favored nation. Christ will be in control of the affairs of earth, gloriously reigning from Jerusalem. And the Jews will serve as His priests and vice regents, in full realization of all that God had promised them.

WHAT ABOUT RUSSIA?

We have examined Israel's unique role among the nations. She had a distinct beginning, for she was singled out by the Lord Himself. To her were given many marvelous promises, some of them conditioned upon her faithfulness to the laws of God. Upon her shoulders were placed numerous responsibilities: she would be the vehicle of God's revelation, she would become the avenue of redemption for all mankind, she would be the people through whom the Messiah-king would be born, and she would be a witness to the world, demonstrating God's holiness and grace.

But this brought her into conflict with the nations. Her high moral standards, monotheistic beliefs, unique sacrificial system, dietary regulations, and refusal to intermarry with surrounding peoples caused her to be hated by her neighbors. Even when she was scattered throughout the countries of the world by God in judgment for her disobedience, her people remained aloof, preferring to live in poverty-stricken ghettos in deplorable conditions rather than lose their natural distinctions. Her principle of passive resistance made her the scapegoat of ambitious Gentile rulers.

Large numbers of Jews migrated to Russia. They seldom had life easy there. The czars humiliated them, taxed them heavily, and used them capriciously to divert attention from their own cruelty. Sweeping purges and terrible pogroms would periodically reduce the Jewish population. At one point, during the 19th century, all people of Israeli descent were herded together to live in wretched conditions in a land area called "the Pale." Russia has seldom if ever treated the Jews kindly.

Sad to say, it is no different in the Soviet Union today. The Jews are often misrepresented and mistreated. They have few opportunities for vocational or material advancement. It's difficult for them to purchase property or own a business. Travel is restricted, and only a few of the older people, no longer able to work, are allowed to emigrate to Israel.

Internationally, Israel's enemies are Russia's friends. When Israel first gained independence, the Soviet Union made repeated overtures for good relationships. But her primary intention—to dominate the Middle East and to have access to oil apart from the Arabs—soon became clear. It wasn't long before Russia withdrew every pretense of friendship and sided with Israel's foes. Since then, the Soviet Union has been actively cooperating with them to the point of providing them with arms, reconnaissance assistance, and military advisors.

It isn't difficult to foresee a day, perhaps

in the near future, when Russia will invade Israel. If she swept down through Iran, her forces could be in the mountains of Judea in weeks or even days. How could Israel ever withstand this kind of military aggression? Apart from the help of God, she would soon fall.

And the Bible teaches that the day is coming when Russia will invade Israel. There is no doubt. The bear *will* move south. Her armies will occupy the highlands of central Palestine and threaten Israel's continued existence as a distinct people. Then, when all hope of survival seems gone, God will intervene. But more of that later.

3
Russia and the Revived Roman Empire

"It shall be in the latter days . . ."

The goals of the Russian Communist are clear: world domination. Lenin, the father of communism in Russia, declared, "As long as capitalism and socialism exist, we cannot live in peace: in the end, one or the other will triumph—a funeral dirge will be sung either over the Soviet republic or over the world of capitalism." Joseph Stalin continued the conflict with the West, stating that the struggle between them would decide the fate of capitalism and socialism throughout the world. And Nikita Khrushchev's famous statement was, "We will bury you." Later he told an American television audience, "Your grandchildren will live under socialism."

Recent events in the lands bordering Russia have caused us to look again at Bible prophecy. Russia's full support of Vietnam's conquest of Cambodia is an ominous sign. So is the zealous band of Communist reactionaries in Iran, supported by the Soviet Union who is determined to take over the new government of the Ayatollah Khomeini. The peace treaty between Begin and Sadat and the threat of Islamic retaliation demand our attention. So does the Russia-China rift.

These startling occurrences, all related to the Soviet Union, raise questions about the days ahead. What does the Bible have to say about the future of the nations? Will Israel survive? What about the rumors of the revived Roman Empire? Where exactly does Russia fit into the jigsaw puzzle of endtime events?

The future of the nations is best understood when the passages that foretell the revival of the Roman Empire are studied and compared. Remember, the fourth nation of Nebuchadnezzar's dream and Daniel's vision has been positively identified by Bible scholars as Rome. In each instance it was depicted as immensely strong and terrible, asserting tremendous influence upon the nations of the earth. Ancient Rome was invincible militarily, controlling vast land areas and people during her heyday. Her sphere of domination extended from Great Britain to the Middle East, from Africa to the borders of Russia. No one could stand against her and hope to survive. Those who dared to challenge her were humiliated and their lands were destroyed. The Jews themselves discovered that in A.D. 70 and again in A.D. 130.

But Rome's days of glory came to an ignominious end. Her moral laxity led to idleness, luxurious living, and widespread immorality. The government became unstable; the military leaders were corrupt and incompetent. By the time her borders began to crumble, her personal integrity and strength were already in ruin. Finally, Rome fell. And western civilization was plunged into 10 centuries of chaos.

The prophecies of Daniel, however, tell of a day when the Roman Empire will come to life again. Corresponding with its re-emergence as a world power will be the unfolding of the endtime events. Israel will play an antagonist's role in the new Rome's plans, and Russia will be a key factor in her rise to power. Therefore, the events among the nations today bear close watching, for they may be the foregleams of the dawn of the final days.

In this chapter we will return to Daniel 2 and 3 for a closer examination of the prophecies about Rome, the fourth world empire. We will also investigate two key passages in Revelation that link the New Testament to the prophecies of Rome's revival. Then we will consider briefly Russia's role in the unfolding events of future history.

NEBUCHADNEZZAR'S DREAM: THE ROMAN CONFEDERATION

In his troubled sleep, the king of Babylon envisioned a huge image with a head of gold, chest of silver, abdomen of bronze, legs of iron, and feet of iron and clay. Here is how Daniel described the dream of Nebuchadnezzar:

> Thou, O king, sawest, and behold a great image. This great image, whose brightness was excellent, stood before thee, and the form of it was terrible.
>
> This image's head was of fine gold, its breast and its arms of silver, its belly and its thighs of bronze,
>
> Its legs of iron, its feet part of iron and part of clay.
>
> Thou sawest until a stone was cut out without hands, which smote the image upon its feet that were of iron and clay, and broke them to pieces.
>
> Then were the iron, the clay, the bronze, the silver, and the gold, broken to pieces together, and became like the chaff of the summer threshing floors; and the wind carried them away, that no place was found for them; and the stone that smote the image became a great mountain, and filled the whole earth (Daniel 2:31-35).

The legs of iron no doubt represent the eastern and western branches of the Roman Empire. It naturally follows that the toes (Daniel 2 doesn't say there are 10, but it follows from the configuration of man) represent 10 nations or groups of people. In his interpretation of the dream, Daniel said,

> And the fourth kingdom shall be strong as iron, forasmuch as iron breaketh in pieces and subdueth all things; and, as iron that breaketh all these, shall it break in pieces and bruise.
>
> And whereas thou sawest the feet and toes, part of potters' clay and part of iron, the kingdom shall be divided; but there shall be in it of the strength of the iron, forasmuch as thou sawest the iron mixed with miry clay.

> And as the toes of the feet were part of iron and part of clay, so the kingdom shall be partly strong and partly broken.
>
> And whereas thou sawest iron mixed with miry clay, they shall mingle themselves with the seed of men; but they shall not adhere one to another, even as iron is not mixed with clay (Daniel 2:40-43).

Nothing has happened in history to correspond with the specific statements of verses 42 and 43. Bible scholars who are literalists therefore believe that the statements about the toes of the feet of the image—of iron and clay that would mingle with the seed of men but not mix—apply to the future. A gap in time exists between verses 41 and 42. From the fall of Rome to its revival in the future is a long, unspecified period that may soon be coming to an end.

Perhaps the best evidence for this time-lapse and the revival of Rome as an empire is found in the following verse:

> And in the days of these kings shall the God of heaven set up a kingdom, which shall never be destroyed; and the kingdom shall not be left to other people, but it shall break in pieces and consume all these kingdoms, and it shall stand forever (Daniel 2:44).

Note that the verse begins, "And in the days of these kings shall the God of heaven set up a kingdom." The kingdom the Lord will set up can only be the millennial kingdom, for it will "never be destroyed" and will "stand forever." But who are "these kings" mentioned in the first part of the verse? The "these" can only refer back to verses 42 and 43, which mention 10 toes as 10 kingdoms.

This links the events of these verses directly to the future kingdom of God. Therefore, the passage must necessarily be speaking of a future Roman Empire—a revived empire of 10 nations, headed by Rome, that will become powerful and oppressive. But it will be internally weak, as symbolized by the incompatible iron-clay mixture. This interpretation fits another key passage, Daniel 7, to be discussed shortly.

Many Bible scholars have attempted to identify these 10 nations specifically, but that is an impossibility. Logic tells us that they will probably come from the vast land areas held by ancient Rome, but we cannot be certain which of them. We do know, however, that Israel will be deeply involved. And, as shall be seen later, we know that Russia will be too—but *not* as one of the nations of the Roman confederation.

DANIEL'S VISION: THE ROMAN PRINCE

We learn more about the revival of the Roman Empire from Daniel's vision of chapter 7 and its interpretation. The prophet saw four beasts: a lion, a bear, a leopard, and a "beast, dreadful and terrible." Daniel described the fourth beast as follows:

> After this I saw in the night visions, and, behold, a fourth beast, dreadful and terrible, and strong exceedingly, and it had great iron teeth; it devoured and broke in pieces, and stamped the residue with its feet; and it was diverse from all the beasts that were before it, and it had ten horns.
>
> I considered the horns, and, behold, there came up among them another little horn, before which there were three of the first horns plucked up by the roots; and, behold,

> in this horn were eyes like the eyes of man, and a mouth speaking great things (Daniel 7:7,8).

The beast had teeth of iron (see Daniel 2) and 10 horns. From among the 10 horns there arose a new "little horn" that plucked out three of the horns, had the eyes of a man, and spoke great things. The Lord explained this part of the vision to Daniel.

> Thus He said, The fourth beast shall be the fourth kingdom upon earth, which shall be diverse from all kingdoms, and shall devour the whole earth, and shall tread it down, and break it in pieces.
>
> And the ten horns out of this kingdom are ten kings that shall arise; and another shall rise after them, and he shall be diverse from the first, and he shall subdue three kings.
>
> And he shall speak great words against the Most High, and shall wear out the saints of the Most High, and think to change the times and the laws; and they shall be given into his hand until a time and times and the dividing of time.
>
> But the judgment shall sit; and they shall take away his dominion, to consume and to destroy it unto the end.
>
> And the kingdom and dominion, and the greatness of the kingdom under the whole heaven, shall be given to the people of the saints of the Most High, whose kingdom is an everlasting kingdom, and all dominions shall serve and obey Him (Daniel 7:23-27).

The 10 horns of this fourth beast represent the 10 kings who will rise to power in the revived Roman Empire of the last days. They correspond to the 10 iron-and-clay toes of the image Nebuchadnezzar saw in his dream (Daniel 2).

The "little horn" signifies a political ruler who will rise to prominence, subdue three rival nations in the process, and soon dominate the other seven. Powerful and arrogant, he will openly defy and blaspheme the Most High God. He will rule for "a time and times and the dividing of time"—prophetic language for 3½ years. Then the judgment of the Almighty will come, and the wicked ruler's kingdom will be destroyed by the "Ancient of days" (v. 22). It will be given to "the saints of the Most High," who will abide forever in faithfulness to the Lord (v. 27). The fall of this "little horn" corresponds to the destruction of the image of Daniel 2 by the stone "cut out without hands" (indicating supernatural activity) that rolls down from the mountains.

The 10 kings represent the rulers of the revived Roman Empire, and are the same as the toes of Daniel 2. Because of their internal weakness (represented by the iron and clay mixture), they will be exploited by an ambitious political ruler, the Antichrist. He will trample over some people on his way to the top. When he ascends the throne of the revived Roman Empire, he will unite it into a powerful political and military force and initiate a program of world domination. Israel will trouble him, and Russia will stand in his way.

REVELATION 13: WORLD DOMINATION

We learn more about the revived Roman confederation and its powerful end-ruler from John's vision of Revelation 13. The apostle wrote,

> And I stood upon the sand of the sea, and saw a beast rise up out of the sea, having

> seven heads and ten horns, and upon his horns ten crowns, and upon his heads the name of blasphemy.
>
> And the beast which I saw was like a leopard, and his feet were like the feet of a bear, and his mouth like the mouth of a lion; and the dragon gave him his power, and his throne, and great authority (Revelation 13:1,2).

The similarities between the description of this passage and Daniel 7 are instantly recognizable. The reference to 10 horns appears in both, as does the indication of the strength and brutality of the creature. The added detail of the seven heads is difficult to interpret, but it may refer to the seven horns that remain after the little horn uproots the other three. It may also represent seven forms of Roman rule, seven successive Roman emperors, or seven Gentile powers that have opposed Israel during the centuries. Whatever the case, they will become insignificant when the little horn rises to power and reduces the others to vassal status.

Several vital pieces of information are included in the first eight verses of Revelation 13 about the new Roman Empire and its tyrannical dictator. A summary of them may be helpful:

1. The beast is like a leopard, a bear, and a lion (v. 2). These are the animals used to symbolize the world powers that preceded Rome in Nebuchadnezzar's dream—Babylonia, Medo-Persia, and Greece. Evidently this kingdom will incorporate the most significant aspects of each of them.

2. It is given Satan's power and authority (v. 2). This terrible beast will enact the devil's will upon the earth, joining the serpent and

Judas Iscariot as those who were "entered into" by Satan. The dragon in Scripture is a clear metaphor for the fallen angel Lucifer.

3. The beast, Antichrist, will stage a resurrection from the dead (v. 3). He will have received a deadly wound, but he will be healed. This apparent miracle will attract the wonder and attention of the world.

4. He will demand worship and receive it (vv. 4,8). His fierce pride and intense evil will drive him until he usurps God's position among the nations. Like Satan, he will not be happy until he assumes God's rightful place of sovereignty (Isaiah 14:12-17).

5. He will blaspheme God (vv. 1,5,6). As he gains in power, his defiance of the Lord of Glory will express itself openly. He will speak derisively against the Lord's name, the Lord's temple, and the Lord's people. His hatred of God will be all-absorbing, and he will despise all that the Lord represents.

6. He will persecute the saints (v. 7). His antagonism against the Lord will be focused upon His people. A great multitude of those who believe in Jesus Christ, both Jew and Gentile, will be put to death because they refuse to bow the knee to this wicked, self-aggrandizing ruler of the revived Roman Empire.

There can be little doubt that this world leader of rebellion against God is Antichrist. Along with his cohort, the false prophet (Revelation 13:11-18), this wicked man will attain global authority. All will fear him. Those who oppose him will be punished without mercy. He will focus his hatred upon the Jews, doing all he can to harass them.

This "false christ" is a real human being who will be vested with the power of Satan himself. Intensely evil, he will be like sin personified. In fact, he is referred to as the "man of sin" in 2 Thessalonians 2:3. Once he has begun his headlong dash down the roadway of evil, he will not stop until he is defeated by the Lord Jesus Himself.

REVELATION 17: RELIGIOUS COUNTERFEIT

A final reference in Scripture to the beast with 10 horns appears in Revelation 17. This scene describes the end of an unholy alliance between Antichrist, who is rising to power as head of the revived Roman Empire, and apostate Christendom. The event no doubt occurs toward the close of the first half of the tribulation. As Antichrist ascends to global prominence, he will be assisted by a corrupt, worldwide religious organization, symbolized by the harlot. She is portrayed as riding the scarlet-colored beast (Antichrist), which shows that her position is founded upon him and that she still has some authority. When he reaches the top, however, all of that changes.

> And there came one of the seven angels who had the seven bowls, and talked with me, saying unto me, Come here; I will show unto thee the judgment of the great harlot that sitteth upon many waters;
>
> With whom the kings of the earth have committed fornication, and the inhabitants of the earth have been made drunk with the wine of her fornication.
>
> So he carried me away in the Spirit into the wilderness and I saw a woman sit upon a scarlet-colored beast, full of names of blasphemy, having seven heads and ten horns.
>
> And the woman was arrayed in purple

> and scarlet color, and bedecked with gold and precious stones and pearls, having a golden cup in her hand, full of abominations and filthiness of her fornication (Revelation 17:1-4).

This wicked harlot, arrayed in the world's finery, represents the uniting of all the world's religions into one vast organization. It will be united with Antichrist's empire, which will be worldwide by this time. Their union will be short-lived, however. According to verse 16, the beast will soon hate the harlot, and will "make her desolate and naked, and shall eat her flesh, and burn her with fire."

Antichrist will thus turn his wrath upon the religious structure that helped him rise to power. He will brutally and shamefully destroy it, leaving himself at the pinnacle of world authority. No one will stand in his way—no one, that is, except that valiant band who believe in Jesus Christ. They will not give in to his godless, immoral way of life, and they will pay a bitter price for their faithfulness to God.

WHAT OF RUSSIA AND ISRAEL?

We have been discussing the nations in the endtimes, particularly during the tribulation. World events will be moving in favor of Satan and his henchmen (or at least it will appear that way). Ten nations will rise to prominence, form a confederation, and become the revived Roman Empire. They will be the fulfillment of major prophetic portions of Daniel and Revelation.

One man, empowered by Satan himself, will force his way into the dominant position of the new Rome. Referred to as "the little horn," the "man of sin," and the "beast," he will hate God and all that He represents. His scheme to dominate the world will achieve universal success.

Several Bible scholars have attempted to identify the 10 nations and their wicked ruler. Some have suggested the countries of the common market in Europe. Others have equated them with the old League of Nations. Still others speak of a new pact by powers occupying lands once amalgamated into the old Roman Empire. But the 10 nations cannot now be positively identified.

We do know, however, that Israel will sign a treaty with the wicked world ruler. A false peace will settle over the land of Palestine. The Israelis will relax their defenses and give their attention to other areas of endeavor. After 3½ years, the peace will be shattered by Antichrist's betrayal of Israel. He will desecrate her temple, turn his fury upon her, and persecute her severely. Israel will cry out to God, and He will bring her deliverance.

I believe the evidence is clear that Russia is *not* one of the 10 nations of the revived Roman Empire. Located far to the North, and never involved with ancient Rome, she has her own distinct place in the prophecies about the nations. As we shall see in the detailed discussion of Ezekiel 38 and 39 to follow, she will most likely stand in the way of Antichrist's ambitions.

This does not mean, however, that she will befriend Israel—not at all! In fact, while Antichrist is busy achieving his goals in Western Europe, Russia will be formulating her own plans for an invasion of the Middle East. Then, at just the right moment, the commands will be given from Moscow. Arms will be taken up. Russian soldiers, prepared and battle-ready, will begin to march. Slowly, invincibly, the bear will move south, finally occupying the very mountains of Israel. In our next chapter we will turn our attention to the nations to the north and to the frightful day when Russia invades Israel!

4
The Russian Bear

"... thou shalt come from thy place out of the north parts"

Bible scholars generally agree that the prophecies recorded in Ezekiel 38 and 39 are about Russia. They foretell in unmistakable terms the day when hordes of armed soldiers from that powerful nation in the far North will invade Israel and occupy the mountains of central Palestine. Only the direct intervention of God will prevent the Israelis living in the promised land from being totally destroyed.

A few short decades ago, this interpretation of Ezekiel seemed like a wild fantasy. The Jews did not live in Palestine but were scattered throughout the world. Russia was a backward, weak, and strife-torn land. Bible scholars were searching for a time in history when the events of Ezekiel 38 and 39 could have happened, but they found none. There seemed to be little chance of their coming to pass in the future. So the prophecies were either spiritualized or somehow lumped in with the cataclysmic events of the day of the Lord.

But modern history has turned these predictions into a probable reality. For one thing, Israel is back in the land as an independent, sovereign nation. She has the backing of the West. She has even made peace with her former enemy, Egypt. Almost as miraculous has been the rise of Russia to the status of a mighty world power. She has moved onto the stage of contemporary international activity with swift and awesome force. No longer underdeveloped and backward, she has a powerful army, growing economic strength, and an unbending, fanatical devotion to her national causes.

It's not really fair, however, to judge all of Russia by today's power-hungry leaders—just as it wasn't in the days of the czars. We cannot understand this nation "out of the north parts" (Ezekiel 38:15) by a brief glimpse of her recent past. In this chapter, therefore, we will take a look at the history, geography, population, and culture of Russia. Our purpose will be to show the nation as it really is, that we might better understand how the prophecies of Ezekiel will be fulfilled.

THE LAND OF THE BEAR

The total area occupied by Russia covers a staggering 8.6 million square miles—one-sixth of the earth's entire land surface. It's the size of the United States (including

Alaska), Canada, and Mexico combined. Latest figures show the population of the Soviet Union to number 258.9 million people. The dominant land feature is a great plain that stretches from the Ukraine to the eastern seaboard, broken only by the Ural Mountains. Russia lies upon the same latitude as Canada. The icy wastes of the north cover huge segments of the land, making them totally unproductive. And vast dry sections in the Siberian regions and south make farming nearly impossible. Therefore, only about 20 percent of the enormous land area of Russia must produce food for the entire nation.

By longitude, Russia stretches halfway around the globe. A trip on the Trans-Siberian Express from Leningrad in the west to Vladivostok on the China Sea takes 9½ days. The country is rich in resources. She's the world leader in iron ore, oil, and magnesium deposits. Her timber reserves and potential water-power supplies are nearly inexhaustible. She is also among the largest producers of coal, lead, nickel, and zinc. But transportation, weather conditions, and a manpower shortage are serious problems yet to be overcome in developing these vast potentials. So is the absence of ice-free ports, which are essential to the easy flow of materials and for reaping the benefits of world trade.

The people of the Soviet Union are made up of more than 175 different ethnic groups, many of whom have retained their language and dialect roots. The population is 55 percent Slavic. The U.S.S.R. is a union of 15 republics, all under the control of the soviet party leaders in Moscow. Systematic purges have kept any attempts at achieving independence under control. The major republics are the RSFSR (the Moscow region), the Ukraine, Byelo-Russia (sometimes called White Russia), and the Trans-Caucasian States (Azerbaijan, Georgia, and Armenia). The Baltic States (Latvia, Estonia, and Lithuania) are important for manufacturing and for their outlet to the North Sea.

Until 1945 the population center was in the west. But the deep inroads of Hitler's troops and the need for rapid development of the raw materials to Siberia have led to a definite eastern shift of population.

To summarize, tractable land has always been a problem in Russia. So have transportation and manpower. The rich resources in minerals and forestry are offset by the lack of productive soil and the difficulties in moving goods. But vast strides forward have been made in Russia since the close of World War II.

A BRIEF HISTORY

The origin of the name "Russia" is obscured by ancient history. The people who first ruled Russia were called the *Rus*, but we don't really know who they were. Some maintain they were Slavic peoples who inhabited the land from prehistoric days. Others maintain that invaders from Scandinavia brought the name with them. Still others say that the Slavic inhabitants referred to the Norse invaders as the *Rus*. We do know that the Greeks used the word "*Rus*" to refer to both Slavic and Norse inhabitants of the Black Sea area. Whatever the case, we cannot be conclusive about the origin of the word "Russia."

The earliest history of Russia is recorded in a work called the *Original Chronicles* by a monk named Nestor (1056-1114). Modern scholars believe that this Kiev historian merely made a compilation of the written records of many generations of historians. Recent archeological discoveries have clarified some of Nestor's material, showing part of it to be accurate but some to be in error.

The history of Russia may be divided into three sections. We will examine each of them briefly.

I. The Rurik Dynasty (862-1598).
II. The Romanov Dynasty (1613-1917).
III. The Bolshevik Revolution (1917).

As we review them, you will see that there has always been a wide gap between the small ruling class and the majority of the population—the peasants. Russia has never known a significant middle class. The serfs, often oppressed and heavily taxed, have remained close to the soil—and in many cases, close to God.

THE RURIK DYNASTY (A.D. 862-1598)

According to the *Original Chronicles* of Nestor, Russia had its beginning as a state in A.D. 862. Legend has it that the Slavic tribes inhabiting the land were in disorder and confusion and desperately needed strong leadership. So they sent emissaries to some Scandinavian people who were called the "Rus Varangian" with this message: "Our land is great and rich, but there is no order in it; come and rule and govern us" (Ivor Spector, *Introduction to Russian History and Culture*, Von Norstrand Press, Princeton, 1961, p. 4). Three brothers led by Rurik, the eldest, took advantage of the opportunity and migrated to Russia. They settled in three different areas, and after their deaths the control of the land was united by Igor, son of Rurik.

This legend, though interesting, is both fuzzy and inaccurate. It is true that the Varangians under Rurik and then Igor did rule, but they probably weren't invited. Furthermore, they most likely moved northward into Russia from the western Black Sea region, not southward. Recent archeological discoveries have shown a distinct Arabic and Semitic influence during these years, also indicating a southern migration.

Christianity arrived in Russia during the early years of the Rurik dynasty. Igor's wife Olga took the throne after he died, and she was converted to Christianity. She was baptized in Constantinople in A.D. 955, and took the Christian name of Helen. She and her son Svyatoslav did not force their people to become Christians, however.

Olga's grandson Vladimir (950-1015), known as the "Grand Prince of Kiev," made Christianity the official state religion of Russia. The Roman and Byzantine branches of the Catholic church competed for Vladimir's favor, along with Mohammedanism and Judaism. The Eastern Orthodox church won out, and a general baptism of the population was ordered in Kiev in A.D. 988-989. Although many Russians had become Christian by Vladimir's day, large segments of the population still held to their pagan beliefs. By 1100, however, orthodox Christianity was firmly established.

The Christian influence was strong in Russia. Architecture, art, and music were shaped by the Byzantine culture. Many scholars say that Christianity is what caused a written language to develop among the Slavic peoples. The nation's moral code was strongly influenced by the church. Education was promoted among the people by religious rulers. A distinctive Christian culture was developing. The clergy played a major role in society, and worship and spirituality were important factors in Russian life. The blossoming of a great new westernized Christian era was about to unfold.

But the entire course of Russian history was abruptly changed. Invading Mongol hordes from the East first threatened the land, then mysteriously withdrew. Seventeen years later they descended in waves upon western Russia. Their military leader was the Genghis Khan, but their efforts were masterminded by a Chinese statesman, Yelu Chu-tsai. By 1243 the Mongols, or "Golden Horde," were in complete control.

Russian civilization suffered under the domination of the rough-living Mongols (or Tartars, as they were also known). Polygamy was practiced by these base eastern conquerors. Slave traffic increased steadily. Women were reduced to near-slave status. The spiritual values of Christian Russia were eradicated. In time, intermarriage even caused a change in the physical appearance of the people. Art, music, and architecture were reduced to primitive forms. All associations with the West, except for purely commercial endeavors, came to an end.

The Russian princes were ruled by Mongol chieftains and taxed heavily, but they waited impatiently for the opportunity to throw off the hated yoke. The church, which before had set such a high spiritual tone, was reduced to being just another powerblock searching for a voice. Gradual assimilation of the original Russians by the Mongols and a general decline in moral life led to increasing brutality and cruelty. Finally, a ruler arose among the Russian princes who was more fierce and bloodthirsty than the invaders—Ivan the Terrible. He was strong enough to break the nation free from the stranglehold of Mongol tyranny and bring Russian rule, no matter how barbaric, back to the land again. But Russia would never be the same. Their own princes had become oriental despots, as cruel as their fierce conquerors. Ivan's death brought complete disorder. Finally a new leader was chosen—mild-mannered Michael Fyodorovitch, the first of the Romanov czars. His family would rule Russia until 1917.

THE ROMANOV DYNASTY (1613-1917)

The years immediately preceding Michael's election as czar are referred to by the Russians as the "Times of Trouble." The Cossacks, outlaw bands of horsemen who lived in southern Russia, made systematic raids on the north. The Swedes and Poles threatened to overrun the land. The princes fought one another in a continual struggle to gain more power for themselves. The age-old enemy of Russia, starvation, threatened the masses. The country was poised between eastern dictatorial practices and western thinking. A strong leader was needed to restore order, unite the people, repel the invaders, and bring an end to suffering and brutality.

Just such a man arose and assumed control in 1682. A member of the Romanov family, he was known in history as Peter the Great, a brilliant, impressive figure. At 6′7″ and 230 pounds, he was a natural leader. The people put their faith in him, and he did not disappoint them. He studied history and learned about the Russia of pre-Mongol days. He soon decided to return to those ideals, and initiated an ambitious program of westernization. In a few short decades (he ruled from 1682 to 1725), he succeeded in making barbaric Russia a cultured European nation once again.

He founded St. Petersburg in 1705 and made it his capital. He overcame the clergy and nobility, created a new aristocracy, promoted education and the sciences, and authorized the construction of factories and mills. His harsh but popular rule turned Russia's face westward, and by the time his reign ended, the nation was a united, growing, pro-Western country.

Some retrogressions followed his death. Foreign influences—German, French, and British—swayed the successive czars. When Catherine II (the Great) took the throne, however, strong leadership returned to the land. She upgraded education, raised the literacy rate, and promoted cultural expression. She was a skilled writer herself, and produced a number of important works. Russian territory expanded significantly to the west and south during her beneficent rule.

One blight remained upon the Russian scene during these years of phenomenal progress. The serfs were kept in abject poverty and humble servitude. They were bonded to the land and had no hope of escaping the few acres of soil assigned to their families. They were taxed heavily and given few rights. Unable to find material happiness, many Russian peasants maintained a firm faith in God and hope of blessings in Heaven.

After Catherine, Russia continued to make progress. The country was given new confidence when its armies defeated Napoleon. The growing nation continued to upgrade her status among the people of western Europe. Finally, in 1861, the serfs were set free from the land, albeit they were granted few opportunities to improve their lot in life. Then the wave of liberalism was slowed down by a reactionary move that crushed the common people. This led to the rise of political parties and the infamous "Bloody Sunday" revolution of 1905. Jews were severely persecuted. The czars and nobles were losing their grip. The old way of life was coming to an end.

Anton Chekhov captured the transitional mood in his famous play, *The Cherry Orchard.* Written in 1903, it portrayed in unmistakable terms the closing days of the nobility and the rise of the new way of life.

The sprawling nation was at a critical point in its history. The decadent, impoverished nobles were hanging on tenaciously to the old way of life—their lavish estates, mannered gentility, abundant servants, and landed wealth. But merchant capitalists were rising throughout the land. The new cry was, "We need less villages and orchards, and more cities, railroads, and factories." In the play, the noble Ranevsky family loved its crumbling manor house and rundown cherry orchard. But Lopakhin, a prosperous merchant, wanted to take possession of the orchard and make suburban villas out of it.

The struggle between the noble family and the merchant was intense, but the outcome was inevitable. The Ranevskys finally ran out of money and Lopakhin purchased the land. As the play ended, the only sound to be heard was the chopping of an axe as the fruit trees started to fall. Nobility was dead. The new order prevailed. Czarism's days were at an end.

Chekhov's play proved to be prophetic. Few could have foreseen the tumultuous events of 1917. The time was ripe for change. The army was demoralized after years of fighting in World War I. The Jews, so often made scapegoats in brutal pogroms, were fearful. The serfs were starving. The country was racked by political strife. The question on every mind was, "Whose star will rise?" The answer came in October of that critical year.

THE BOLSHEVIK REVOLUTION (1917)

When Russia went to war against Germany in 1914, it was with a poverty-stricken population and disorganized government. The demands of all-out military effort demonstrated clearly the failures of the czarist regime. No firm, visionary leadership was offered. Conditions worsened. Upheaval was inevitable.

Finally the turning point came. Contrary to popular impressions, the Bolshevik revolt was far from a well-planned and smoothly run coup. False starts, bad decisions, and near-sighted thinking nearly quenched the movement before it began. The revolution actually started in March of 1917 with a general strike of 200,000 in St. Petersburg, accompanied by street fights. This led to a revolt by the czar's regiments and the arrest of his cabinet. A provisional committee was established in Moscow under a four-party coalition. Political prisoners, including a revolutionary named Joseph Stalin, were released. A neutral transitional government was formed, headed by Kerensky. When the czar abdicated, Nikolai Lenin traveled to the Soviet Union, bringing 80 million German Marks with him to finance the communist endeavor.

By June, however, the first Bolshevik revolution had failed. Leon Trotsky returned from the United States with solid financial backing for the anti-communist provisional government. But the Bolsheviks would not be discouraged and continued to make gains in district and city governments. Sensing the inevitable, Trotsky decided to join them. Lenin, who had been forced into exile in July, returned secretly to the Soviet Union in October. The pro-Bolshevik Red Army was formed, and on November 6, Lenin emerged from hiding to demand an immediate uprising. The next day the Bolsheviks seized power and the provisional government came to an end.

Anti-communist forces rallied, and a "white" army was formed to resist the "reds" of the Bolsheviks. Lenin severely purged the government and strengthened his control throughout the land. The "whites" held out for 3 years, but were poorly organized and meagerly funded. They received little help from outside, and they gave up in 1920. Amazingly, a free election had been held in Russia on November 25, 1917, and there had been a substantial anti-communist majority!

An assassination attempt on Lenin's life in 1920 led to the first "Red Terror," a purge of unbelievable proportions. The opposition was all but liquidated.

The year 1921 saw the death of Lenin and the rise of Stalin. A marked increase in religious persecution followed. Trotsky was removed from power and exiled in Mexico, but he was murdered on orders from Stalin. The strong-armed dictator assumed full control, and in 1933 he instituted a fierce purge in which 1.5 million of his own party members were put to death.

The beginning of World War II brought a temporary end to religious persecution and the beginning of severe economic difficulties in the Soviet Union. When Hitler invaded Russia in 1941, he was offered massive support by the Russian citizens. Unfortunately, his secret police were soon as cruel to the people as Stalin's henchmen had been, so they withdrew their support. I strongly believe they are still looking for a leader who would grant them political and religious liberty, equality, and just laws.

These significant events followed the Allied victory over Germany:

1945-48 Russia annexes the Eastern European satellite countries except for Yugoslavia.

1952 Land reforms produce some positive results.

1953 Joseph Stalin dies and Nikita Khrushchev rises to power. He presents his famous "different roads to Communism" speech, indicating a softening of the hard-line position.

1956 De-Stalinization begins in earnest in Russia. Yet Khrushchev says of the

West, "History is on our side. We will bury you."

1959 Khrushchev redefines communism as follows: "Communism means that a man should have good clothing and a good place to live so that people can learn, work with self-denial for the good of society, and make use of the achievements of science, culture, and art."

1960 Khrushchev's Christmas Day speech: "Our rocket has passed the moon. It is already approaching the sun, and we still haven't discovered God. We have now snuffed out lights in the heavens that no man will be able to rekindle. We are engaged in breaking the yoke of the gospel, the opium of the masses. Let us only proceed, and Christ will speedily be relegated to mythology."

1961 Khrushchev's "New Policy" program. He continues to attack the memory of Stalin, creating a rift with Red China.

1962 The Cuban missile crisis weakens his hand at home and abroad.

1964 Khrushchev is ousted for repeated agricultural failures. Brezhnev replaces him, and reinstitutes a radical Marx-Lenin doctrine.

The past 15 years gradually have produced a return to Khrushchev's "peaceful co-existence" attitude toward the West. Under Richard Nixon's initiation, a mutual policy of detente was established. Meanwhile, the Russo-Chinese rift has steadily widened. Repeated crop failures have forced the Soviet Union to be dependent upon the West for wheat. A major anti-Christian purge took place in 1973 and Russian Jews have continued to suffer. Since 1973, the Soviet Union has initiated a new offensive in world domination, centering in Africa and Southeast Asia.

RUSSIAN CULTURE

To provide a balanced view, let us look at some of the cultural achievements of Russia. Her people have produced much great literature, art, and music. Her most productive years were known as the "Russian Renaissance" of 1840-1905.

Writers

A brief survey of her great authors follows:

Pushkin was Russia's first great modern writer. His penetrating short stories pointed out the plight of the peasants and contributed to later reforms. His work did much to unify and define the Russian language.

Gogol continued Pushkin's work. His *Dead Souls* (1842) decried the evils of serfdom and the pitiable human beings it produced. He turned to a new theme with the publication of his most important work, *The Cloak*. Here he pointed out the insensitive brutality of the aristocracy. A poverty-stricken peasant worked for years to purchase a cloak, yet the first night he wore it, it was arrogantly stolen by a nobleman. The poor man was helpless to retaliate—depicting the true condition of the Russian serfs.

Turgenov produced in his *Memories of a Sportsman*, a Russian *Uncle Tom's Cabin*. It had a devastating effect upon society, for it exposed the true state of serfdom.

Dostoevsky. This brilliant nationalistic author pointed up the dangers of westernization, especially in his great novel *Crime and Punishment*. Raskulnikov, his hero, is influenced by the liberal ideas of Voltaire and Rousseau, and he murders an evil old pawnbroker. The novel also is an intense, pre-Freudian essay on the psychological effects of crime. *The Brothers Karamazov* was an epic novel on Russian life. The first brother, Dimitri, represented the old-line nationalists; Ivan, the free-thinking westerner; the retarded Smerdyakov, the mob; and the spiritual Alyosha, the potential savior of Russia. Tragically, the novel was not finished, so we do not know Dostoevsky's solution to his country's ills.

Tolstoi was an immensely wealthy nobleman who accepted Christianity. He sold nearly all his possessions and wandered throughout Russia, giving his money away to the poor. His great novel *War and Peace* shows all facets of Russian life.

Chekhov published *The Cherry Orchard* in 1903. As noted above, it demonstrated the decayed glamour of the crumbling aristocracy and the inevitable advance of a new way of life.

Pasternak wrote during the more liberal Khrushchev era. His most famous work, *Doctor Zhivago,* offered hope for the Russian common man. It was smuggled out of Russia and published in Italy.

Solzhenitsyn published novels depicting life in Soviet prisons during the Stalin era. *The First Circle* and *Cancer Ward* were devastating exposés, as was *A Day in the Life of Ivan Denisovitch. Gulag Archipelago* on the same theme, did not achieve the greatness of his earlier works.

Composers
Included among the great musicians of Russia are:

Moussorgsky, an early composer who presented a realistic interpretation of music.

Rimsky-Korsakov, who composed numerous liberal works including an opera that was banned for speaking against the state.

Tchaikovsky, a nationalist who composed pieces to capture the beauties of Russian landscapes, customs, and achievements. His famous "1812 Overture" immortalized the defeat of Napoleon. His grand symphonies were on the theme of man versus fate.

Stravinsky is a modern composer who returned to the theme of Russian nationalism.

The contribution of the Russian writers, composers, and artists to world culture has been significant. Since 1917, however, most have worked with themes dictated by the state (as the poem "Bratsk Station"). Those who dared write of human freedom have excelled, but have had to publish underground. They have been oppressed and have faced terrible persecution. Solzhenitsyn's secretary, for example, committed suicide after telling where her private copy of his novel was hidden. She had been questioned and tortured for 5 days without sleep before she broke.

COMMUNISM

A consideration of Russian history and life could not be complete without at least a brief look at Communism. Although the Russian government leaders are of this persuasion today, only about 3.5 percent of the population are true party members. If the common people, descendants of the serfs of the czarist days, really had their way, it is certain that they would never choose to be ruled by the Communists.

Communism is a "utopian" doctrine. It proposes to create a "heaven on earth." This goal is to be achieved through the equal distribution of wealth and income, and through common ownership of property. Karl Marx and Rudolf Engels first presented this theory in their book *Communist Manifesto*, published in 1848. They based their theory upon the newly formed social sciences. They saw the rising industrial class as the key to establishing their new order, and they dared to cry for worldwide revolution. They wrote:

> The Communists disdain to conceal their news and arms. They openly declare that their ends be attained only by forcible overthrow of all existing social conditions. Let the ruling class tremble at the Communistic revolution. The proletariat (common people) having nothing to lose but their chains. They have a world to win. (Karl Marx and Rudolf Engels, *Manifesto of the Communist Party*, 1848).

Later Marx elaborated, saying,

> The worker must one day seize power in order to erect the new organization of labor; he must push to one side the old politics which uphold the old institutions, if he does not want to suffer the loss of heaven on earth, as did the old Christians who are neglected and despised. (Karl Marx, *Address at the Hague Congress*, 1872).

It was Vladimir Ilyich Ulyanov (alias N. Lenin) who saw the economic unrest of Russians as the basis for political upheaval. He formed the Social Democratic Party during the waning years of the czars. He saw insurrection as the only means of achieving his goals and instituted the following five rules for successful revolt by the masses:

1. Mean business. Don't stop until you succeed or die.
2. Amass superior forces.
3. Being on the offensive is fundamental. "The defense is death to an insurrection."
4. Surprise is basic.
5. Moral superiority is vital *(Encyclopedia Britannica,* Vol. 6, p. 206).

Once in power, Lenin insisted a dictatorship is the only viable means of government for communism. "Violence wins revolution: dictatorship assures it," he wrote. Only a dictator true to the party could be trusted. The worst of Lenin's philosophy was realized in Joseph Stalin. No one has counted the millions who died, even including many faithful Communist party members, during his fierce purges of 1935-1939. Interestingly, his henchman Khrushchev, the "butcher of the Ukraine," did not carry out his policies when he came into power. And, except for a brief relapse in 1973, neither has Brezhnev. One can only wonder at the policies of the strong men who will succeed the ailing party leader.

CONCLUSION

We have taken a look at Russia's history, her people, her leading authors and composers, and her cultural development. The pattern remains constant: the large majority of Russian people throughout the centuries have been oppressed, tyrannized, and forced to live in poverty. The bright flame of hope in the early 20th century when the czars fell soon turned to despair when the Bolsheviks took control. The czars had merely been replaced by the Communists; a cruel minority again controlled the wealth of the nation. The hopeless status of the common people did not change.

No one knows when the prophecies of Ezekiel 38 and 39, speaking of a Russian invasion of Israel, will take place. But the Communists, now in control, have long hated the Jews. They have repressed and despised them. Their atheistic doctrine is diametrically opposed to belief in God. The Jews are therefore natural enemies, an enmity intensified by their radical commitment to Judaistic traditions.

I feel a great sadness for the Russian people. One can only wonder what they really are like—and what they would become if ever granted freedom from totalitarian oppression. I'm beginning to think the world will never know.

5
The Bear Goes South

"I will bring thee forth . . ."

Things are happening rapidly in the Middle East. The Shah has fallen from power in Iran. With the United States as mediator, Israel and Egypt, bitter antagonists for the past 30 years, have signed a historic peace treaty. The Arab extremists have had their way in laying down a strict boycott of Egypt, their previous ally. The price of oil keeps inching upward, contributing to an alarming, worldwide inflation. Perhaps it is the Arab world's means of punishing the pro-Israelis. Yes, day after day, the world's attention is focused upon the cradle of God's prophetic program, Palestine and her neighbors.

Bible prophecies that seemed incredible only a few decades ago have become frighteningly possible. Until the close of World War II, for example, many Bible scholars scoffed at the idea of a literal fulfillment of Ezekiel 38 and 39. After all, the Jews were still scattered among the nations, with only a small percentage living in Palestine. The holy land itself was under Arab domination. Meanwhile, far to the north, the Russian bear was still in hibernation. World War I had demoralized her population and decimated her armies. The Bolsheviks were experiencing one economic and agricultural failure after another. The nation was lagging far behind the West in industrial growth, development of resources, and military capabilities.

But now all of that has changed. Israel is back in the land as an independent nation. She successfully defended her independence in 1948 and has been victorious in two major wars since. Her presence is a vital factor in all Middle East affairs. Then too, Russia has burst upon the international scene as a major world power. The nation's recovery from the devastation of World War II has been rapid and complete. She now rivals the United States in sophisticated weaponry, industrial output, and space technology. The stated goal of her Communist leaders—world domination through economic revolution—has never been retracted. And Israel stands in the way of the realization of her plans in the Middle East. If Iran should fall under Soviet domination, the gateway would be open for a military drive into the oil-rich fields of the Arab countries and fertile plains of Palestine. Yes, today a Russian invasion of Israel is far from an impossibility; in reality, it could happen very soon.

As one who interprets the Bible literally,

I am convinced that the day is coming when Russia will invade Israel. The prophecy of Ezekiel, I believe, clearly indicates that the bear will move south into the promised land. Russian troops will encamp on Israeli soil, and the little Jewish state will be in grave danger. Therefore, in this chapter and the next, we will look at Ezekiel 38 and 39 in depth. We will examine the prophecies carefully, analyze them in terms of today's world, and consider what role these events play in God's overall plan for the endtimes.

PRELIMINARY OVERVIEW

The 38th and 39th chapters of Ezekiel are a single unit. The section divides naturally into the four divisions, each beginning with a command from the Lord for the prophet (interestingly, referred to in each instance as "son of man") to prophesy (see 38:2, 14; 39:1,17). Three times Ezekiel was told to address Gog of the land of Magog, and in the fourth he was instructed to speak to "every feathered fowl, and to every beast of the field" (39:17). The entire prophecy is spoken against the warlike ruler of a nation located in "the north parts."

The prophecy is composed of three basic elements: invasion, destruction of the invaders, and resulting carnage. First, the *invasion* of Palestine by Russia is inevitable. Gog, the prince of Magog, will unite with several other countries to arm and train a great military force. They will then "come like a storm" (38:9) into Palestine and march "against the mountains of Israel" (38:8). They will cover the land "like a cloud" (38:9), threatening to overrun the tiny nation of the

Jews on their way to other conquests in Africa and the Middle East.

A second element of the prophecy recounts how the Lord will destroy the invading hordes. Fury will rise up in the face of Jehovah, and a great shaking will rock the camp of Israel's fierce enemy (38:19,20). Israel's foes will turn their swords upon one another. Then God will send pestilence, rain, hailstones, and fire upon them. The invaders from the north will be destroyed.

The remainder of Ezekiel's message of chapters 38 and 39 describes the carnage that will result from the destruction of the northern confederation. Discarded weapons will provide fuel for 7 years (39:9,10). It will take 7 months to bury the bodies of the dead (39:12). God will call carnivorous birds and animals to take their fill, and all will be satisfied. God's name will be magnified in it all, for Israel and the nations will be given undeniable evidence that He is the Lord (39:21,23).

Two basic interpretations of these chapters have been presented by Bible expositors. The first, propounded by liberal scholars, calls for a figurative interpretation of Ezekiel 38 and 39. The references to an invasion and the great destruction of the foreign armies are seen as imaginative representations of the Bible concept of the end of time. Whoever wrote it (these scholars do not believe it was Ezekiel) merely wanted to exalt the name of Jehovah through stunning apocalyptic descriptions. The unknown penman, they say, was merely finding a graphic way to communicate his concept of the power of Jehovah.

Bible scholars of the fundamentalist tradition, however, have always maintained that the events depicted in these chapters will take place as stated. Armies from the far north *will* invade Palestine, and they *will* be destroyed by the supernatural intervention of God. Great numbers of enemy soldiers *will* occupy the mountainous regions of Palestine. After their destruction at God's hand, it *will* take many months to bury their bodies. The awesome events of Ezekiel's prophecy (he truly is the author) will occur at some future time in human history, and exactly as he predicted.

The Bear Goes South is written from the standpoint of a literal interpretation of Scripture. Even the most jaded skeptic will agree that the stage of international politics is set for the events Ezekiel described. What seemed impossible a few short years ago could actually happen. But numerous questions arise if one is to accept the literal viewpoint. Who is Gog? Where is Magog? When in God's program for the endtime will these events take place? What will be their effect on the unfolding drama of Israel's restoration? To find the answers, we turn now to a consideration of the prophecy in detail. As we work through it, we will see the solution to these basic questions.

THE INVADERS IDENTIFIED

Our first task is to identify with certainty the people responsible for this large-scale invasion of the promised land. Ezekiel named them as follows:

> And the word of the Lord came unto me, saying,
>
> Son of man, set thy face against Gog, of the land of Magog, the chief prince of

> Meshech and Tubal, and prophesy against him,
>
> And say, Thus saith the Lord God: Behold, I am against thee, O Gog, the chief prince of Meshech and Tubal,
>
> And I will turn thee back, and put hooks into thy jaws, and I will bring thee forth, and all thine army, horses, and horsemen, all of them clothed with all sorts of armor, even a great company with bucklers and shields, all of them handling swords:
>
> Persia, Cush, and Put with them; all of them with shield and helmet;
>
> Gomer, and all its hordes; the house of Togarmah of the north quarters, and all its hordes, and many peoples with thee (Ezekiel 38:1-6).

The evidence is overwhelming that the leader of the attacking nations is Russia. No other region fits the information included in the prophecy as well. Three lines of argumentation may be followed to make the identification positive.

1. *The Geographic Designation.* Ezekiel said that these armies would descend from the north. The Hebrew words do not mean simply somewhere close, as St. Louis is north of Memphis. Rather, they could more accurately be rendered "the uttermost parts of the north." This phrase occurs three times in the passage. In 38:6, therefore, the house of Togarmah is in the uttermost parts of the north. In 38:15 we are told that the armies will come from their place out of the "north parts." And in 39:2 it is recorded that God will cause the invaders to come down from the north parts.

In biblical terminology, compass directions are always in relation to Palestine (called, significantly, the center or "navel" of the earth in Ezekiel 5:5). A line drawn from Jerusalem to the North Pole would pass almost directly through Moscow. Besides, the sprawling nation of Russia lies directly north of any area in the Middle East. Only the land currently occupied by the Soviet Union, therefore, qualifies as being to the far north of Israel.

Furthermore, as noted in a preceding chapter, Magog has long been identified with Russia. In Genesis 10 he was identified as the second son of Japheth. Josephus, the renowned Jewish historian of New Testament days, identified Magog with the Scythians. These ancient peoples originally settled north of Israel and later migrated all the way northward to the Arctic Circle. Jerome also stated that the Jews used this term to designate the Scythian tribes to the north.

Three pieces of geographic evidence therefore point directly to Russia as the future invader of Israel: (1) the term "north parts," which occurs three times in the prophecy, (2) the fact that Russia lies directly north of Palestine, and (3) the ancient identification of Magog with the Scythians, who we now know migrated throughout Russia and settled near Moscow.

2. *Anthropological Evidence.* In the opening of the prophecy, Ezekiel named the leader of the invasion force as "Gog, of the land of Magog." Evidently this person designated as "Gog" is the ruler of a land called "Magog."

A number of theories have been presented to identify Gog. Some have said that the word sounds like it should fit Antichrist, but nothing in Scripture indicates this. Others have said this name was simply a derivation of the name of the country, Magog. This cannot be, however, for the name also appears in 1 Chronicles 5:4. True, the Egyptians used the word "Gagia" to designate certain barbaric tribes, but there is no link between their use of the term and the word that appears in Ezekiel 38.

Further evidence of his identity is found in verse 3, where Gog is called the prince of Rosh, Mesheck, and Tubal. The Hebrew word *rosh* can mean "head" or "first" (as in *rosh hoshannah,* the "head of the year"), but the indications here are that it is a proper noun like "Meshech" or "Tubal." As we have seen, from ancient days the word *Rus* has been used to identify the inhabitants of Russia. The change from *rus* to *rosh* could easily occur over the passing of time. Many leading linguistic scholars, including the brilliant Gesenius, are convinced that our word "Russia" was derived from the early term *rosh.*

Not coincidentally, the words "Meshech" and "Tubal" are also similar to some familiar Russian words. "Meshech," for example, sounds very much like "Moscow." And "Tubal" is similar in sound to the important province Tobolsk, located in eastern Russia.

Admittedly, these designations could be questioned. *Rosh,* for example, may mean "head" or "chief" in this passage. Meshech could refer to the Moschi peoples, identified by early writers as the inhabitants of Phrygia in Asia Minor. And Tubal could be the ancient Tibareni peoples of Cappadocia. But when one links the invaders from the far north with the Scythians, and when one notes the similarity of the names of verse 3 to age-old Russian designations, there can be little doubt that Russia is the nation that will invade Palestine.

Perhaps a word needs to be said about the nations that will confederate with Russia in the invasion (see vv. 5,6). Persia, of course, is modern-day Iran, the scene of a recent political upheaval. With the Shah ousted, the country is now in the hands of the Moslem priest Khomeini. But his regime is not without opposition. Communist-inspired rebels were out of his control during the coup, and have been difficult to handle since then. All during the uprising, for example, they broadcast a steady stream of anti-American propaganda into the country and called for an immediate end to all Western influence. It appears they have succeeded in their goal. Now with the departure of the Americans, it will be easier for them to cause trouble when the 79-year-old patriarch dies. If the Communists gain control, Russia will be almost at Israel's back door.

"Cush" (v. 5) is an old name for Ethiopia, also the site of recent Communist uprisings. In fact, they have gained control of the government. "Put," usually identified as Libya, is already in the Arab bloc of nations and lined up against Israel.

"Gomer" (v. 5) refers to the Cimmerians, well-known ancient tribes that settled along the Danube and Rhine Rivers. They became part of the Germanic peoples, many of whom are now under the control of the Soviet Union.

Finally, "Togarmah" (v. 6) is a reference to the Armenians, who once lived directly north of Israel but later migrated up into the Caucasus region. They too have been taken over by the hammer and sickle.

Ezekiel's message is clear. With Russia as ringleader, a great upheaval will one day threaten the Middle East. Armed hordes from the north will push into Palestine, assisted by confederates from the west and south. Alarmingly, each of the nations Ezekiel named is currently either part of the Soviet Union or threatened by her. The stage is set for this aspect of the prophecy to be fulfilled.

3. *Religious Consideration.* A third indication that the invasion will come from Russia can be inferred by an examination of their attitude toward God. The invaders will obviously have no respect for the Lord, nor for His people, the Jews. Ezekiel wrote that Gog would "think an evil thought" (v. 10)—the plunder of Palestine. Without regard for the Jews as God's beloved people, and with no thought of anything but enriching himself at Israel's expense, the Russian ruler will march his forces across their borders. He will very likely have no concept of the importance of Palestine in God's program. The promises of the Bible will be unknown to him. Driven by greed, he and his armies will enter the land "like a cloud," prepared to take the wealth of Israel for themselves.

The similarities between Gog's purposes and methods and those of the Communists can readily be demonstrated. Communistic ideology calls for a worldwide takeover of all human and natural resources. The means of achieving their goals is through revolution of the masses, armed invasion and occupation, and strong dictatorial rule. The Poles, Czechs, Hungarians, Lithuanians, Estonians, Latvians, Afghans, East Germans, Bulgarians, Cambodians, Koreans, and Cubans can testify to the success of this method with dismayed, helpless voices.

Every nation today needs oil to survive. It therefore takes little imagination to picture the military, economic, and political importance of the Middle East. Very soon, it could be that whoever controls this area will dominate the world. For a nation that has already shown in frightful terms that a takeover by armed forces is part of their national strategy, marching into the Middle East seems only natural. The gateway is Israel, and modern Russia fits the biblical description of the invaders exactly. It seems to me that the question is no longer *if,* but *when.* We turn now to a discussion of the time in God's prophetic program when that northern invasion will take place.

THE TIME OF THE BATTLE

Enough information is presented by the prophet to give us a good idea of when this all-important battle will occur. Bible scholars have suggested three possible times: (1) Some say it will occur during the tribulation period, but before Christ's glorious return. (2) Others, on the basis of the description of conditions in Jerusalem when the invaders come, locate it during the millennial kingdom. (3) Still others, linking this passage with the reference to Gog and Magog in Revelation 20, say that the invasion will occur during that short season when Satan is released after the 1,000-year reign of Christ is completed.

When we evaluate the information given in this passage, we can only conclude that the Russians will invade Israel sometime during the tribulation period, the first of the views mentioned above. Three key facts contribute to this conclusion:

1. *The Location of the Prophecy.* Contrary to the opinion of some current scholarship, Ezekiel is indeed the author of chapters 38 and 39. The style is his, as is the familiar designation "son of man." Furthermore, the passage fits in the general flow of prophetic events being described in the latter section of Ezekiel. Chapter 34 condemns the faithless rulers of Israel. Chapter 35 speaks out against Israel's enemies in Edom. The first part of the next chapter describes the return of the Jews to Palestine. The remainder of chapter 36 and the crucial "dry bones" chapter, 37, depict Israel's future spiritual restoration—her acknowledgment of the Messiah and her national return in faith to the Lord. Then comes the account of the northern invasion in chapters 38 and 39. A lengthy description of the glorious temple to be established during the millennial kingdom concludes the book (chapters 40-48).

This pinpoints the Russian invasion as occurring during the tribulation. It will take place after Israel's return to the land (chapters 36,37) but sometime before the beginning of the millennial kingdom (chapters 40-48).

2. *The Time Designation.* The prophet was very conscious of the time reference of his prophecy, and this is the second reason for designating its fulfillment as during the tribulation. He referred to the "day" of its fulfillment on several occasions (38:8,14,19; 39:8,11). The phrase "in the latter years" appears in 38:8, and "in the latter days" is in 38:16. This expression is significant whenever it occurs in the Old Testament, or when its equivalent is used in the New. When it is mentioned in a prophecy, it refers specifi-

cally to messianic times—events related to the return of Jesus Christ and His kingdom. It speaks precisely of that day when God's attention will again be upon Israel, and when she will fulfill His program for her upon the earth.

The focus of Ezekiel 38 and 39 is specifically upon Israel during the endtime events. All attempts to find an instance in history that would correspond to these prophecies end in failure. They still await fulfillment.

3. *Conditions in the Land.* Ezekiel described what conditions will be like in Palestine when these events take place. This provides us with a third reason for placing their fulfillment during the tribulation.

> After many days thou shalt be visited; in the latter years thou [Gog] shalt come into the land that is brought back from the sword, and is gathered out of many peoples, against the mountains of Israel, which have been always waste; but it is brought forth out of the nations, and they shall dwell safely, all of them.
>
> And thou shalt say, I will go up to the land of unwalled villages; I will go to those who are at rest, who dwell safely, all of them dwelling without walls, and having neither bars nor gates,
>
> To take a spoil, and to take a prey; to turn thine hand upon the desolate places that are now inhabited, and upon the people that are gathered out of the nations, who have gotten cattle and goods, who dwell in the midst of the land (Ezekiel 38:8,11,12).

A close examination of these crucial verses unveils several factors that pinpoint with startling accuracy when the invasion will occur.

First, we know it will happen while Israel

is occupying the promised land. According to Ezekiel, the Jews will have been reassembled in Palestine from all parts of the earth, for he said they would be "gathered out of many peoples" (Ezekiel 38:8). Then, in verse 12 he said these things would happen to a people "gathered out of the nations."

From the destruction of Jerusalem in A.D. 70 until the rise of Zionism in the 20th century, the Jews were indeed scattered among the nations of the earth. Very few lived in Palestine until the end of World War II. When the nation declared independence in 1948, Jews began to immigrate to Palestine in large numbers. From 1 million in 1948, their number has swelled to nearly 4 million today. They are a sovereign nation, they have their own flag, they speak their own language, and they have successfully defended their own borders. The land is flourishing, and the nation is economically strong. In the past 30 years, we have witnessed the rebirth of the ancient nation. Her people have assembled from all over the world.

Second, the invasion will come when the Jews have built flourishing, open cities. The prophet wrote that Gog, commander of the northern armies, would say this of his decision to attack:

> I will go up to the land of unwalled villages; I will go to those who are at rest, who dwell safely, all of them dwelling without walls, and having neither bars nor gates (Ezekiel 38:11).

A journey through Israel today would take you through numerous new settlements. They don't have thick walls like cities of ancient days. There are no massive gates with heavy metal bars. What good would they be against modern warfare anyway?

I believe more is intended, however, than simply a description of cities without walls. The basic concept is of a people at peace. They are unafraid; they are "at rest" (v. 11). They dwell in safety (v. 14). There will be no need for walls and gates, for no one will expect attack. A sense of security will pervade the land.

Third, the prophecy will be fulfilled at a time when Israel is enjoying material prosperity. The invaders will be after her silver and gold, her cattle and goods (v. 13). In fact, if the attack were to be successful, they would take back a "great spoil." A few short years ago, no one would have wanted Palestine for her wealth. Her rocky soil, mosquito-infested swamps, and arid lands were anything but prosperous. The return of the Jews, however, has changed all that. By great effort and self-sacrifice they have made the land flourish. Rich farmlands now stand where unproductive soil lay before. The chemicals of the Dead Sea are being mined, processed, and sold for profit. Vast natural resources are becoming available in abundance. Exports exceed imports in numerous commodities, particularly citrus, cut diamonds, and textiles. Fertile soil that only needed water to become productive is now being utilized to produce abundant crops.

Something more may be involved in the "great spoil" the invaders are after. It could well be that their primary objective is control of the vast oil resources in the Middle East. In a number of ways, Israel is the key that unlocks the treasury of Middle East oil reserves. Right now her strong militia precludes any strong-arm tactics by foreign influences in the entire region. Whoever attempts to bully the oil nations has to think about her air superiority, her sophisticated and highly mobilized weaponry, and her crack troops. But if Israel's military is taken out of the picture, then foreign aggression instantly becomes more of a probability. World domination through the manipulation of oil would be the primary objective.

In summary, the text of Ezekiel 38 and 39 gives us sufficient evidence to identify the Russians and pinpoint when their invasion of Israel will occur. We know that it will happen in the "latter years," a phrase that always refers to messianic days. We also know that *the bear will move south* sometime after Israel has been regathered from among the nations of the world, which we have seen in our lifetime. Furthermore, it will be a time of safety and prosperity in Israel. The cities won't be strongly defended and much spoil will be there for the taking. All of this points forward to the endtimes. We will discuss exactly how the Russian invasion fits into God's prophetic program in the next chapter. But another penetrating question—God's purpose for allowing the battle—must be discussed beforehand.

DIVINE PURPOSE FOR THE BATTLE

Some of the verses of Ezekiel's prophecy against Russia literally drip with divine irony. Speaking to the northern hordes, the Lord said through the prophet,

> Be thou prepared, and prepare for thyself, thou, and all thy company that are

> assembled unto thee, and be thou a guard unto them (Ezekiel 38:7).

How ironic! Here is God warning Gog to be prepared for any eventuality. But no amount of preparation will save the invading armies from the destruction that awaits them. The more men they equip and bring south, the more devastating their losses will be.

The Lord Himself will be the motivating factor in Russia's decision to cross Israel's borders. He will turn them aside from their original objective and bring them into Palestine, like a fish being directed through the water with a hook in its mouth (38:4). Later in the passage the Lord told Gog, "*I* will bring thee against *My* land" (v. 16).

Yes, the Lord Himself will direct Gog's forces to the mountains of Israel. And when they are entrenched there, He will destroy them. Why will He do so? What will be His purpose and objective? The text itself gives us some idea.

To Fulfill Prophecy. Long before Ezekiel received this revelation from God, the former prophets of Israel had written of these events. Twice their writings are referred to in the passage. Speaking of Gog in chapter 38, the Lord said,

> Art thou [Gog] he of whom *I have spoken of old* by My servants, the prophets of Israel, *who prophesied in those days many years* that I would bring thee against them? (Ezekiel 38:17).

Then, in the next chapter, Ezekiel wrote,

> Behold, it is come, and it is done, saith the Lord God; this is the day *of which I have spoken* (Ezekiel 39:8).

No prophecies that name Gog and Magog specifically were written before this time. We must therefore conclude that the general prophecies about the destruction of Israel's enemies, issued beforehand, apply in this case. Several passages describe the judgment of God upon the ungodly nations, and these are certainly what Ezekiel must have had in mind (see Psalm 2; Numbers 24:17-24; Daniel 2:44, 45; and Joel 3).

To Judge Russia. God is not ignorant of Russia's program for world domination. He knows that the basic doctrines of Communism call for global conquest through revolution. He also knows how many Jews have lost their lives behind the iron curtain, and how many have suffered severely at the hands of cruel oppressors. He knows too that the people of the satellite nations are being repressed and tyrannized.

He also knows that Communism is atheistic. Not only does it not believe in God; it is vigorously anti-God. Wherever it takes control, its ruthless leaders do all they can to quench the fires of the Christian faith. Churches are closed, meetings are forbidden, and evangelistic efforts are outlawed. Believers are denied good jobs and harassed in other ways. So opposed to Christ is Russian Communism that its leaders will jump at the chance to invade the promised land of God's chosen people.

But when they do, they will be making a terrible mistake. Ezekiel says the anger of our omnipotent, righteous God will rise up in His face (Ezekiel 38:18). He will pour out His wrath upon these enemies of Israel. The very mountains they occupy will shake, fire and brimstone will fall from Heaven, and the armies will be destroyed. The patience of God with a belligerent, disobedient nation will run out, and in His fury He will purge the mountains of Palestine of the foreign invaders.

REVIEW

Ezekiel's prophecy is sure. The day is coming when Russia will invade Israel. At some future time her armies will pour down into Palestine and blanket the land. The Israelis, back in their land after a great regathering and living in safety and prosperity, will be faced with extinction. But God will intervene to destroy the fierce invaders. His purpose will be carried out in exact detail.

But a number of questions about the terrible days described in Ezekiel 38 and 39 remain unanswered. We turn now to a more thorough examination of the prophecies and a consideration of the role their fulfillment will play in God's overall program.

6
Russia's Defeat in Israel

"I will turn thee back . . ."

The avowed purpose of Russian communism is world domination. Her vast land areas are rich in the raw materials essential for war. She has a sophisticated and deadly arsenal of weapons, including advanced nuclear devices. She has swallowed up one country after another. Her sphere of influence reaches throughout Africa, into Southeast Asia, and even to the Western Hemisphere. She has a population of 258.9 million and one-sixth of the earth's land resources.

It hardly seems fair that she would attack Israel, a postage-stamp-sized country of less than 4 million. Yet at some time in the future, perhaps very soon, it will fit into Russia's plans to invade and plunder Israel.

Her troops will swarm into Palestine. Very likely her strategy will be to control Israel first then take over the entire Middle East with its vast oil reserves. She would then be in the position to force the whole world to its knees.

But the Bible teaches that she will never achieve her ambitious goals. Her invasion of Palestine will be smashed by the direct intervention of the Lord of Glory. So, Israel doesn't need to fear the Russian bear. The Scriptures indicate that only four nations will rule the world, and Russia is not one of them (see Daniel 2 and 4). Ezekiel 38 and 39 tell us that the Russians are headed for a shattering defeat. It seems that God will tire of the blasphemy and atheism of the Soviet Union, and He will send a devastating judgment upon her from on high.

In this chapter we will look closely at Ezekiel's account of Russia's bold invasion of Israel, and we will note the dire outcome. We will locate this event in the unfolding timetable of the prophetic future, finding significant connections with the era preceding Christ's second coming. We will also answer a number of perplexing related questions about the future. And we will analyze the overall effect of the battle, seeing how God's name is exalted in it all.

Yes, there's no doubt about it. The fierce Russian bear *will move south.* She will become a frightening menace to God's chosen people. But the Lord God will intervene on Israel's behalf. And when He does, the bear will turn tail and go running.

THE INVASION DESCRIBED

Ezekiel 38 and 39, twin accounts of the same

prophetic events, describe the invasion of Israel by the northern confederation. Chapter 38 records the details of the attack itself.

> After many days thou [Gog] shalt be visited; in the latter years thou shalt come into the land that is brought back from the sword, and is gathered out of many peoples, against the mountains of Israel, which have been always waste; but it is brought forth out of the nations, and they shall dwell safely, all of them.
>
> Thou shalt ascend and come like a storm; thou shalt be like a cloud to cover the land, thou, and all thy hordes, and many peoples with thee.
>
> Therefore, son of man, prophesy and say unto Gog, Thus saith the Lord God: In that day when My people of Israel dwell safely, shalt thou not know it?
>
> And thou shalt come from thy place out of the north parts, thou, and many peoples with thee, all of them riding upon horses, a great company, and a mighty army;
>
> And thou shalt come up against My people of Israel, like a cloud to cover the land; it shall be in the latter days, and I will bring thee against My land, that the nations may know Me, when I shall be sanctified in thee, O Gog, before their eyes (Ezekiel 38:8,9, 14-16).

Gog will arm and mobilize a huge army for all-out war. Russian troops, supported by soldiers from Iran, Ethiopia, Libya, and parts of Eastern Europe, will begin their move southward.

Apparently their original purpose will *not* be to march against Israel. Some other goal will be in their minds—most likely the conquest of the oil-rich lands of the Middle East region. But the Lord will turn them aside and draw them into Palestine (38:4). Whatever their original objective, it will be forgotten in their greed.

Although it is the Lord who brings the northern hordes into Israel, Satan will be involved as the motivating force. His hatred of God and His people has not changed, nor will it ever. He'll be delighted that an "evil thought" has come into Gog's heart, and he will rejoice when the Russian leader decides to divert his forces into the promised land (38:10,11).

That which will sidetrack Gog is pure greed. Israel will have become a rich nation by the time this military operation begins. She will be very wealthy, as indicated by Ezekiel's reference to her silver, gold, cattle, and goods. The assets of Israel have already multiplied many times since the austere days of her declaration of independence. Though her defense commitments are large, she is becoming a prosperous nation. Fertile soil, rich mineral reserves, industrial capabilities, and capital investments are increasing her wealth steadily.

As Gog's troops move southward, he will reason, "Why not take Israel? Her defenses are thin. Her people are relaxed and safe." Ezekiel stated Gog's specific purpose bluntly: "To take a spoil, and to take a prey" (38:12). The greedy heart of the northern ruler will desire Israel's wealth, and he will give orders to his troops to "take a great spoil" out of Palestine (38:13).

At first it will appear that his plan is succeeding. His huge army will march into Israel with little opposition. He will easily occupy the mountains of central Palestine, his forces poised for the kill. With a simple command, the entire land would swiftly become his.

GOD'S SUDDEN INTERVENTION

The Lord's patience has run thin with Israel many times in her history. With full justification, He has often used the nations of the world to punish His chosen people. First it was Assyria, then Babylonia. Later the Romans brought terrible destruction, scattering the Jews throughout the entire earth for hundreds of years. Down through the centuries, medieval warlords, petty rulers, czars, megalomaniacs like Adolf Hitler, and cruel dictators like Joseph Stalin and Nikita Khrushchev have persecuted the Jews mercilessly. When Russia's troops are in central Palestine, it will look like God is about to deal His disobedient nation a final, crushing blow of judgment.

Just at the critical moment, however, the Lord will intervene on Israel's behalf. His purpose will not be her destruction, but her salvation. He will have brought the invading armies of the northern confederation into the mountains of Judea to destroy *them*—not Israel. It is against Gog that the fierce anger of the Almighty will be kindled, and He will pour out His wrath upon him and his armed forces with unspeakable fury. Ezekiel wrote,

> And it shall come to pass at the same time when Gog shall come against the land of Israel, saith the Lord God, that My fury shall come up in My face.
>
> For in My jealousy and in the fire of My wrath have I spoken, Surely in that day there shall be a great shaking in the land of Israel,
>
> So that the fish of the sea, and the fowls

of the heavens, and the beasts of the field, and all creeping things that creep upon the earth, and all the men that are upon the face of the earth, shall shake at My presence, and the mountains shall be thrown down, and the steep places shall fall, and every wall shall fall to the ground.

And I will call for a sword against him throughout all My mountains, saith the Lord God; every man's sword shall be against his brother.

And I will enter into judgment against him with pestilence and with blood; and I will rain upon him, and upon his hordes, and upon the many peoples that are with him, an overflowing rain, and great hailstones, fire, and brimstone (Ezekiel 38:18-22).

The description of God's fury rising up in His own face (v. 18) is like a man who becomes extremely angry. A similar phrase appears in Psalm 18, where David wrote,

Then the earth shook and trembled; the foundations also of the hills moved and were shaken, because He was angry.

There went up a smoke out of His nostrils, and fire out of His mouth devoured; coals were kindled by it (Psalm 18:7,8).

The Lord will be angry with Russia. We can only speculate that He has had enough of their oppressive cruelty, their hatred of His holy name, and their violence against His chosen people. He will *not* let the soldiers of this cruel northern confederacy plunder the Jews.

Ezekiel pointed out that God Himself will destroy Israel's enemies. He will not use a secondary agent, but He will send His own supernatural judgments upon them in several forms. First, there will be "a great shaking in the land of Israel" (Ezekiel 38:19). Tremendous earthquakes will rock the land with such violence that mountains will be thrown down, steep places will fall, and buildings will crumble.

Second, a general panic will grow into wild anarchy among the invading troops. As was the case on several Old Testament occasions, the enemies of God will turn their swords upon one another (see 2 Chronicles 20:22-25 for an example).

Third, crippling diseases will rage through the armies, for God will "enter into judgment against him with pestilence and with blood" (v. 22). Hundreds of thousands of Gog's men will die in the earthquakes, great numbers will slay one another, and millions more will fall victim to the horrifying diseases that always accompany war.

Fourth, many who live through these cataclysmic events will die in an awesome display of natural catastrophes. God will send a devastating rain of fire and brimstone, perhaps more dreadful than a nuclear explosion, to decimate the remaining troops of the northern armies.

When all of this Divine activity is ended, the mighty force of evil will be crushed and broken. Ezekiel described Gog's plight as follows:

> And I will smite thy bow out of thy left hand, and will cause thine arrows to fall out of thy right hand.
>
> Thou shalt fall upon the mountains of Israel, thou, and all thy hordes, and the peoples that are with thee; I will give thee

> unto the ravenous birds of every sort, and to the beasts of the field to be devoured.
>
> Thou shalt fall upon the open field; for I have spoken it, saith the Lord God (Ezekiel 39:3-5).

Gog's armies will have fallen in the field, their weapons useless. The northern leader himself will lie dead. His power to dominate and plunder the Middle East will have been destroyed by the intervening hand of God the Almighty.

A COMPLETE DESTRUCTION

The prophet, as spokesman of God, used three graphic word pictures to describe the totality of Russia's destruction. A look at each of them separately will benefit our discussion.

1. *The Discarded Weapons.* Evidently the armies of Gog will number in the millions, for they will leave behind a huge amount of weapons. The prophet described what the Jews will do after the battle is over.

> And they that dwell in the cities of Israel shall go forth, and shall set on fire and burn the weapons, both the shields and the bucklers, the bows and the arrows, and the handspikes, and the spears, and they shall burn them with fire seven years,
>
> So that they shall take no wood out of the field, neither cut down any out of the forests; for they shall burn the weapons with fire; and they shall spoil those that spoiled them, and rob those that robbed them, saith the Lord God (Ezekiel 39:9,10).

Think of it! Enough fuel will be supplied by the discarded armies of the northern confederation to keep the fires of Israel burning for 7 years!

Perhaps it would be well to digress for a moment here to discuss a question that has long bothered Bible scholars. Will these actually be wooden spears and arrows, or was the prophet speaking metaphorically? Those who want to interpret the passage literally give one of the following reasons for saying the weapons will be made of wood: (1) A treaty outlawing modern weapons will have been signed and enforced, so that wood is all the Russians could use. (2) Because of highly sensitive devices used to detect metal, the invaders will use wood to gain the advantage of surprise. (3) The scarcity of fossil fuels will have forced the Russians, who have the world's largest forest reserves, to rely upon armaments fashioned out of wood and transported by horses (this could be the reason for her invasion of the Middle East—to acquire sorely needed oil).

Other Bible scholars say that the prophet obviously was speaking in terms the people of his day would understand. What could Ezekiel know of present-day rockets, tanks, and heavy artillery? These soldiers will be fully armed with the best of modern weapons—that's what Ezekiel really meant. "But," someone asks, "how can they be used for fuel?" Consider for a moment. If this vast army, carried in motorized troop-carriers and fortified by tanks and mobile missile launchers, were suddenly reduced to nothing, huge supplies of gasoline and oil would be left behind. These could later be reclaimed and used by the Israelis to heat their homes and run their factories. But whatever the case, to leave behind this much material for fuel, a huge army will have been destroyed.

2. *The Long Burial Period.* A second indication of the extent of the destruction is the abnormally long period of time it will take to clear the land of the bodies of the fallen soldiers. Citizens of the Middle East have always felt that the earth is corrupt until the dead are buried. This was the case with ancient Israel, and it will be true of the future inhabitants of Palestine as well. Therefore, they will want to inter the corpses as quickly as possible. But so many will have died that it will be a monumental task. Ezekiel wrote,

> And it shall come to pass in that day, that I will give unto Gog a place there of graves in Israel, the valley of the travelers on the east of the sea; and it shall stop the noses of the travelers, and there shall they bury Gog and all his multitude; and they shall call it the Valley of Hamon-gog.
>
> And seven months shall the house of Israel be burying them, that they may cleanse the land.
>
> Yea, all the people of the land shall bury them; and it shall be to their renown on the day that I shall be glorified, saith the Lord God.
>
> And they shall set apart men for the continual task of passing through the land to bury, with the help of the travelers, those that remain upon the face of the land, to cleanse it; after the end of seven months shall they make their search.
>
> And the travelers that pass through the land, when any seeth a man's bone, then shall he set up a sign by it, till the buriers have buried it in the Valley of Hamon-gog (Ezekiel 39:11-15).

The burials will be done "east of the sea," probably in the valley of the Jordan just above the Dead Sea. It will take 7 months to complete the task. Diverted from his original purposes to plunder Israel, Gog himself will have become the spoil. And the Lord's people, as they purify the land, will marvel at His power and glory. They will rename the valley Hamon-gog, which means "plunderers of Gog." Rather than carrying off the spoil of Israel, the northern invaders themselves will lie buried in the ground.

3. *The Feast of Birds and Animals.* In a passage eerily reminiscent of Revelation 19:17,18, the Lord God will call carnivorous birds and beasts to Palestine from everywhere to take their fill upon the fallen soldiers of Gog.

> And, thou son of man, thus saith the Lord God: Speak unto every feathered fowl, and to every beast of the field, Assemble yourselves, and come; gather yourselves on every side to My sacrifice that I do sacrifice for you, even a great sacrifice upon the mountains of Israel, that ye may eat flesh, and drink blood.
>
> Ye shall eat the flesh of the mighty, and drink the blood of the princes of the earth, of rams, of lambs, and of goats, of bullocks, all of them fatlings of Bashan.
>
> And ye shall eat fat till ye be full, and drink blood till ye be drunk, of My sacrifice which I have sacrificed for you.
>
> Thus ye shall be filled at My table with horses and chariots, with mighty men, and with all men of war, saith the Lord God (Ezekiel 39:17-20).

With frightful irony, the Lord will call the birds and beasts of prey to a sacrificial feast. It will be held at His table (v. 20). The passage describes in vivid terms the extent of the destruction and certainty of the judgment so justly deserved. The armies of Gog, well-fed and confident, will become the victims of a sacrifice of greed. A holy and righteous God will be the exalted host of a banquet for birds of prey, and His name will be glorified in all the earth.

This will be God's battle. No Israeli soldier will fire a shot. No innocent Jewish women or children will die. God will speak, and the destruction of the invaders will be terrible and complete. And, the door of prophetic history will be opened to the concluding scenes of the tribulation.

PLACE IN GOD'S PROPHETIC PROGRAM

Obviously, the events described by Ezekiel are of supreme significance. The elimination of a major power like Russia from the scene of international politics will have far-reaching implications. But when will it happen? We have already learned that the invasion by the northern confederation headed by Gog will take place in the last days (38:8,16). Let us now see if we can determine exactly when it will occur. As we examine the evidence, we will find that the aftermath of Russia's collapse will be even more dreadful for Israel—and all mankind—than the event itself.

Three major views concerning the fulfillment of the prophecies in Ezekiel 38 and 39 have been set forth. We have previously discounted the possibility that they have already come to pass, for nothing in history even vaguely parallels the prophet's description. One group of Bible scholars holds the position that the fulfillment will come sometime during the tribulation, probably near the midpoint. A second says that it will occur early in the millennium. And a third pinpoints it after the 1,000-year reign, when Satan is released for a short season. A consideration of each of these views follows, in the reverse order of listing.

After the Millennium. Those who say Russia's invasion of Israel will take place after the 1,000-year reign of Christ base their reasoning on two factors. The first is the description of Israel's peace and prosperity. These conditions, they say, will certainly characterize the Jews at the close of Christ's millennial reign and during the brief period of Satan's release to follow (Revelation 20:7-10). The second consideration is that Gog and Magog are mentioned in that passage. It reads:

> And when the thousand years are ended, Satan shall be loosed out of his prison,
> And shall go out to deceive the nations which are in the four quarters of the earth, Gog and Magog, to gather them together to battle; the number of whom is as the sand of the sea.
> And they went up on the breadth of the earth, and compassed the camp of the saints about, and the beloved city; and fire came down from God out of heaven, and devoured them.
> And the devil that deceived them was cast into the lake of fire and brimstone, where the beast and the false prophet are, and shall be tormented day and night forever and ever (Revelation 20:7-10).

Dr. M. R. De Haan has given four good reasons why the Gog and Magog of Revelation 20 *cannot* be the same as those mentioned in Ezekiel. They are summarized as follows:

1. The Gog of Ezekiel comes only from the north, but in Revelation 20, the armies that

are assembled will come from the four corners of the earth.

2. The word "Gog" may also mean "prince." The leader of the northern invaders is a ruthless Russian dictator, while the armies of Revelation will be led by Satan himself, the "prince of this world."

3. In Ezekiel, the northern ruler is against the nation of Israel, and God is against him. In Revelation, however, the evil prince is against God Himself, and against the saints gathered in Jerusalem.

4. Ezekiel states that the armies of Russia will be destroyed upon the mountains of Israel. Only a small remnant will escape and make their way back home; the rest will be destroyed by the sword, pestilence, and fire, and be buried in Palestinian soil. In Revelation 20, however, no swords are drawn and no time is given for disease to strike. With startling suddenness, fire will come down from God out of Heaven and devour them (Revelation 20:9). The enemies of God will be plunged alive to their doom (De Haan, M. R., *Signs of the Times,* Zondervan, 1951, pp. 90,91).

These considerations clearly indicate that the invasion from the uttermost north will *not* take place when Satan is loosed at the close of the millennial reign of Christ.

Early in the Millennium. The Russian march into Israel cannot be during the years when Christ is ruling the world in peace and righteousness from the throne of David in Jerusalem. Those who hold this view can point to the prophetic description of conditions in Israel at the time of the battle as evidence for their position. The biblical depiction of life during the 1,000-year reign seems to fit with Ezekiel's statements about unwalled cities, rest, safety, and prosperity in the land of Palestine.

But an armed invasion could not occur during the early days of the millennium. It just doesn't fit the general description of the time involved. Besides, Christ would know of the scheme and would stop the armies before they could start moving. So just and complete will be His rule that no nation will be able to take up arms without His knowing it. The prophet Isaiah stated clearly that there will be no war in the messianic kingdom (Isaiah 2:4). The true safety of the reign of the Prince of Peace will not be broken by the sound of marching feet, the crackle of rifle fire, or the rumble of cannon.

During the Tribulation. When the evidence is weighed carefully, the only time the northern invasion could occur is during the tribulation, Daniel's 70th week (Daniel 9:27). "But," you say, "how can that be? Ezekiel said the invasion will occur when Israel is at peace and feels safe. Isn't the tribulation supposed to be an era of terrible wars, supernatural judgment, and seething turmoil?" No, not all of it—as we shall see.

The Bible teaches that after the church is raptured (taken to be with Christ), a leader will emerge to head up the revived Roman Empire. He will be a counterfeit christ (the Antichrist, also called the "man of sin" and the "prince that shall come"). According to Daniel, he will sign a 7-year treaty with Israel. Lulled to complacency by his false peace, the Jews will slacken their defenses. They will evidently divert most of their defense budget into peacetime causes. New cities, unfortified because of the treaty, will probably be built. No doubt foreign trade will increase and production will rise. The tiny nation, free from exorbitant defense spending, will prosper as never before.

For the first 3½ years of that treaty, Israel will be at peace, become wealthy, and feel secure. The evidence is that the Russian invasion will take place toward the close of this first half of the tribulation. Shortly after Russia is defeated, Antichrist will break his treaty with Israel by desecrating the temple. This act will initiate 3½ years of terror for God's chosen people. The evil world ruler will focus his hatred of the Lord upon her.

If this interpretation is valid, and I believe it is, then a number of mysteries about the endtimes are cleared up. For one, why will Antichrist make a treaty with Israel in the first place? I believe it's because his plans for world domination are being thwarted by Russia. He cannot afford to go to war in the Middle East because he is occupied with expanding the realm of his influence, and with fending off the threat of communism. He knows the Russian bear will only let him go so far.

It could well be that he and Gog will be bitter rivals. The oil of the Middle East may be the focal point of their antagonism. The northern confederation, fearful of losing the struggle, may actually begin moving its troops into that area for the express purpose of controlling the flow of oil. But Gog is greedy. He will stop to plunder Israel on his way to his other, more significant objectives. But that decision will bring about his downfall.

With Russia out of the way because of the Lord's intervention, Antichrist will make his move for world domination—and he'll achieve great success. He won't need the treaty with Israel anymore. His fierce anti-God feelings will lead him to desecrate the temple and break the pact. He will soon gain control of much of the earth. Palestine will become his playground, and he'll march his armies into the land. Few will be left to oppose him. He'll be unstoppable until he turns his blasphemous fury upon the believing Jews. At the critical moment, Christ's return in power will save them. Antichrist's forces will be destroyed. Satan will be bound, Christ will ascend the throne in Jerusalem, and a thousand years of peace and prosperity will settle upon the earth (see Revelation 19:11-21).

ANOTHER CONSIDERATION

Some Bible scholars have equated Gog and Magog with the "king of the north" mentioned in Daniel 11.

> And at the time of the end shall the king of the south push at him [Antichrist]; and the king of the north shall come against him like a whirlwind, with chariots, and with horsemen, and with many ships; and he shall enter into the countries, and shall overflow and pass through (Daniel 11:40).

The northern king mentioned here cannot be the same as the Gog of Ezekiel 38 and 39. For one thing, the enemy of the king of the north in Daniel 11 is not the Jews, but Antichrist (Daniel 11:36). For another, the northern king will be joined by two other kings in their attempt to stop the ruthless drive of the willful king toward world domination (v. 44).

In addition, the timing is wrong. Israel's land will already have been torn by the ravages of war. All semblance of peace and safety will have disappeared several years before—the moment the temple was desecrated. The reference here, therefore, must be to the closing months of the second half of the tribulation. The battle of Armageddon and the return of Christ is imminent. Therefore, the northern ruler of Ezekiel cannot be the same as the "king of the north" of Daniel 11:40.

Who then is the northern ruler referred to by Daniel? It could be the leader of the remnant of the Russians who survive the devastation of Ezekiel 38 and 39. They may be recovered enough to mount at least a token attack upon their old enemy, Antichrist. More likely, however, it will be some future ruler of the land previously occupied by Assyria. This seems to fit with parallel prophecies.

RESULT OF THE CONFLICT

As one studies Ezekiel 38 and 39 carefully, he is overwhelmed by the presence of God in the passage. It is the Lord who will "put hooks" into the jaws of Gog and bring him into Israel (38:4). It is the Lord who causes his armies to encamp in the mountains of Palestine. It is the Lord who pours out His wrath upon them. Why is this? What is God's purpose anyway?

The prophet gave us plenty of evidence. Over and over again he said that God's intention will be to use Russia's aggression to magnify His own name among the nations. It will also contribute to Israel's spiritual cleansing and restoration. God said through Ezekiel,

> Thus will I magnify Myself, and sanctify Myself; and I will be known in the eyes of

> many nations, and they shall know that I am the Lord (Ezekiel 38:23).

A little later the prophet wrote these words of the Almighty:

> And I will send a fire on Magog, and among those who dwell securely in the coastlands; and they shall know that I am the Lord.
>
> So will I make My holy name known in the midst of My people, Israel, and I will not let them pollute My holy name anymore; and the nations shall know that I am the Lord, the Holy One in Israel (Ezekiel 39:6,7).

The Lord summed it up as follows:

> And I will set My glory among the nations, and all the nations shall see My judgment that I have executed, and My hand that I have laid upon them.
>
> So the house of Israel shall know that I am the Lord, their God, from that day and forward (Ezekiel 39:21,22).

For centuries the rulers of the world have refused to acknowledge the Lord of Glory. But He will not always tolerate the wicked disregard of His holy name by the nations. He will not let His chosen people suffer at the hands of godless leaders forever. He is sovereign ruler over all. One day, perhaps soon, He will demonstrate His glory to the nations. His judgments will fall, so that His name might be exalted. The journey southward into Israel by the ferocious bear, Russia, will serve that very end.

God will also use that event to exalt His name in Israel. Some time after the defeat of Gog—before 42 months have elapsed—Israel nationally will turn in faith to the God of Abraham, Isaac, and Jacob. She will acknowledge Jesus Christ as the true Messiah. She will put her trust in Him and believe. For a time this will incur Antichrist's fierce wrath, but it will ultimately result in Israel's cleansing, her return to God's favor, and her glorious reign with Christ as His vice-regent and her people serving as privileged priests in the messianic kingdom.

7
The Meaning of Russia's Defeat

"... so the house of Israel shall know that I am the Lord"

The headlines will probably read something like this:

RUSSIAN ARMIES SMASHED
IN PALESTINE

The storyline may go as follows:

> The heavy concentration of Russian troops encamped in the mountains of Israel were suddenly and completely destroyed. The few soldiers staggering back to the homeland tell an almost unbelievable tale of soldiers turning upon one another, of fire raining down from the skies, of thousands

dying in earthquakes, and of raging disease killing their comrades.

The watching world is stunned by this sudden turn of events. The nations had trembled in fear when armed Russian columns crossed the borders of Iran and Turkey a few weeks ago. Their target seemed to be Saudi Arabia and Yemen, the major sources of oil for the Western nations and Japan.

Mysteriously, however, the battle plan changed. The armies veered westward and, without encountering serious opposition, quickly occupied the mountainous heartland of Israel. The doom of the tiny nation seemed imminent. Then, astonishingly, a series of terrible catastrophes befell the huge armies of the north, reducing them to a handful. The entire world breathed a sigh of relief as the decimated forces began to struggle homeward.

Although this account is fictional, it accurately portrays what will happen in the Middle East. Ezekiel 38 and 39 describes in graphic detail the invasion by the northern confederation, their occupation of the mountains of Palestine, and their dramatic defeat.

But the destruction of the Russian armies will not come at the hands of crack Israeli artillery units, nor by the pinpoint bombing raids of F-15 fighters and Mirage jets. Rather, God Himself will intervene, sending a series of calamities which will bring ruin to the invaders. Vast numbers of soldiers will fall in the field, and only a few will escape. The remainder will become carnage for birds and beasts, then be buried in Israeli soil.

The fall of Russia will open the door to the

terrible wrath and devastation of the tribulation. So often rebellious and proud, the nations that began with Noah's three sons will stagger under the crippling blows of cruel dictatorship, rampant anarchy, and Divine chastisement. The "times of the Gentiles," once so filled with hope and promise, will come to a humiliating end. The Lord of Glory will be given great honor, and His chosen people will finally experience the years of abundant blessing God had promised them.

In this concluding chapter we will survey what the Bible teaches about the destiny of the nations. First, we will trace Antichrist's rapid rise to power once Russia has been eliminated. We will then discuss Armageddon, the greatest war of all history. We will consider the biblical teaching about the judgment of the nations, and then look at the coming millennial kingdom to be ruled by the King of Righteousness.

THE WESTERN RULER TAKES CHARGE

We have already discussed the great image Nebuchadnezzar saw in a dream that was interpreted by Daniel (see Daniel 2). Four mighty kingdoms arose to power and then fell. They have been positively identified as Babylon (the head of gold), Medo-Persia (the shoulders and chest of silver), Greece (the thighs of bronze), and Rome (the legs and feet of iron and clay). These nations will have all had their day.

But Scripture also teaches that the Roman Empire will be revived in the last days. The feet and toes, made up of an iron-clay mixture, represent a unique endtime phenomenon. When we link this prophecy with

Daniel 4 and other significant passages, we can only conclude that the day is coming when Rome will again be a world leader. An emperor more powerful and wicked than Caesar, Nero, or Diocletian will sit upon the ancient throne.

Though he will first appear as a prince of peace (a deliberate counterfeit of Jesus Christ), this evil ruler's real goal is world domination. But Israel will stand in his way, and so will the powerful nation of Russia. He will sign a 7-year treaty with Israel and will bide his time with the northern confederation. Just when Antichrist may be getting impatient, Russia's greed will give him his big opportunity. As we have seen, the Soviets will invade Palestine and will be devastated by the Lord Himself. This very likely will give the ruler of the western confederacy (whom we have identified as Antichrist) the chance he's been looking for. With Russia out of the way, he'll initiate his program of world domination.

Without warning, he'll break his peace treaty with Israel by desecrating her temple. Then, with few to resist him, he'll demand worldwide allegiance and servitude. He'll finally show his true colors as a man of unparalleled cruelty and violence. Granted the dominion, power, and authority of Satan himself (Revelation 13:1), he'll focus his hatred upon the Jews and upon all who have placed their trust in Jesus Christ. He'll persecute them fiercely, but the judgment of the Almighty upon him will be even more terrible. Revolution will sweep over the entire globe, bringing death to countless numbers. Millions more will perish in raging pestilences, famines, earthquakes, floods, and other natural disasters.

The Bible teaches that many Jews will believe on Christ during the tribulation, and they will resist the evil leader of the revived Roman Empire. Blind with rage at their stubborn refusal to worship him, Antichrist will order his troops into Palestine. Meanwhile, his stranglehold on the world will begin to weaken. He'll hear of rebellion in the South. An army will be raised in the North. He'll hear rumblings of revolt from the East that will trouble him. Daniel graphically describes these fearsome days as follows:

> And at the time of the end shall the *king of the south* push at him; and the *king of the north* shall come against him like a whirlwind, with chariots, and with horsemen, and with many ships; and he shall enter into the countries, and shall overflow and pass through.
>
> He shall enter also into the glorious land [Palestine], and many countries shall be overthrown, but these shall escape out of his hand, even Edom, and Moab, and the chief of the children of Ammon.
>
> He shall stretch forth his hand also upon the countries, and the land of Egypt shall not escape.
>
> But he shall have power over the treasures of gold and of silver, and over all the precious things of Egypt; and the Libyans and the Ethiopians shall be at his steps.
>
> But tidings out of the east and out of the north shall trouble him; therefore, he shall go forth with great fury to destroy, and utterly to sweep away many.
>
> And he shall plant the tabernacles of his palace between the seas in the glorious holy mountain; yet he shall come to his end, and none shall help him (Daniel 11:40-45).

Apparently Antichrist will successfully withstand these armed attempts to dethrone him. Made bold by his smashing victories, he'll turn his fury upon the saints. Firmly entrenched in Jerusalem, he'll set up his headquarters near the Mount of Olives. His specific goal will probably be the elimination of the 144,000 Jewish evangelists whose fearless preaching and Divine protection will have been a source of embarrassment to him (see Revelation 7:4-8; 14:1-5).

Antichrist's armies, composed of soldiers from all nations, will take up their positions in the plain of Megiddo. Blinded by Satan and driven by hatred for God, they'll make ready for the final rebellion against God. John described it as follows:

> And I saw three unclean spirits, like frogs, come out of the mouth of the dragon, and out of the mouth of the beast, and out of the mouth of the false prophet.
>
> For they are the spirits of demons, working miracles, that go forth unto the kings of the earth and of the whole world, to gather them to the battle of that great day of God Almighty.
>
> And they gathered them together into a place called in the Hebrew tongue Armageddon (Revelation 16:13,14,16).

The stage will be set for the final battle between Antichrist and God's people. At the decisive moment, Jesus Christ will return in glory with the armies of Heaven and do battle with the forces of the evil Western ruler. Zechariah described what will happen:

> Behold, the day of the Lord cometh, and thy spoil shall be divided in the midst of thee.
>
> For I will gather all nations against

> Jerusalem to battle; and the city shall be taken, and the houses rifled, and the women ravished; and half of the city shall go forth into captivity, and the residue of the people shall not be cut off from the city.
>
> Then shall the Lord go forth, and fight against those nations, as when He fought in the day of battle.
>
> And His feet shall stand in that day upon the Mount of Olives, which is before Jerusalem on the east, and the Mount of Olives shall cleave in its midst toward the east and toward the west, and there shall be a very great valley; and half of the mountain shall remove toward the north, and half of it toward the south.
>
> And the Lord shall be king over all the earth; in that day shall there be one Lord, and His name one (Zechariah 14:1-4,9).

The book of Revelation describes the fate of Antichrist (called the beast) and his cohort:

> And the beast was taken, and with him the false prophet that wrought miracles before him, with which he deceived them that had received the mark of the beast, and them that worshiped his image. These both were cast alive into a lake of fire burning with brimstone (Revelation 19:20).

When Antichrist is crushingly defeated by the returning Savior, the revived Roman Empire will collapse forever. The day of the tribulation will be at an end, and the "time of the Gentiles" will be fulfilled. No more will the nations rise up in rebellion against God. No more will people live in unjust and oppressed conditions. No more will the reason, order, and peace of God-fearing rulers be shoved aside by cruel power-hungry dictators. In the millennial kingdom, every nation will acknowledge the Prince of Peace as their rightful King. They'll send their emissaries to worship the Almighty at the altars of the New Jerusalem. The restored and believing Israelites will be their priests. The nations will be governed justly and fairly, overseen by Christ Himself. Peace will settle over the entire earth, and mankind will enjoy 1,000 years of prosperity, safety, and righteousness.

THE JUDGMENT OF THE GENTILES

Before the glorious era of blessing comes upon the world, however, the Lord will judge the Gentiles. He had already punished the nations as *nations*. Remember, God had raised them up for a purpose. They were His divinely appointed means of ruling over the earth, of establishing an orderly and safe environment, and of punishing wrongdoers. But they had failed on every count. Russia had felt His wrath upon the mountains of Palestine. And the world powers experienced His fierce anger during the tribulation and at Armageddon.

Now He must complete the task, focusing His attention upon those Gentiles who survived the tribulation. This judgment will occur at the close of the tribulation, the concluding days of the "times of the Gentiles" (Luke 21:24). It is neither the judgment of the saints nor the final judgment of all men at the great white throne. It's a judgment of the Gentiles—a necessary purging of the earth in preparation for the millennial reign of Jesus Christ. The Lord Jesus described it as follows:

> When the Son of man shall come in His glory, and all the holy angels with Him,

then shall He sit upon the throne of His glory.

And before Him shall be gathered all the nations; and He shall separate them one from another, as a shepherd divideth his sheep from the goats.

And He shall set the sheep on His right hand, but the goats on the left.

Then shall the King say unto them on His right hand, Come, ye blessed of My Father, inherit the kingdom prepared for you from the foundation of the world.

Then shall He say also unto them on the left hand, Depart from Me, ye cursed, into everlasting fire, prepared for the devil and his angels;

For I was hungry, and ye gave Me no food; I was thirsty, and ye gave Me no drink;

I was a stranger, and ye took Me not in; naked, and ye clothed Me not; sick, and in prison, and ye visited Me not.

Then shall they also answer Him, saying, Lord, when saw we Thee hungry, or athirst, or a stranger, or naked, or sick, or in prison, and did not minister unto Thee?

Then shall He answer them, saying, Verily I say unto you, Inasmuch as ye did it not to one of the least of these, ye did it not to Me.

And these shall go away into everlasting punishment, but the righteous into life eternal (Matthew 25:31-34, 41-46).

The time of this judgment is given in verse 31, "When the Son of man shall come in His glory. . . ." This can only be Christ's glorious return to earth to defeat Satan and set up the 1,000-year kingdom.

The place of the judgment is earth, not Heaven. Christ "shall come in His glory," and He will "sit upon the throne of His glory" (v. 31). This is the fulfillment of the earthly rule of Christ predicted by the prophets. Jeremiah's prophecy will come true on the earth:

> Behold, the days come, saith the Lord, that I will raise unto David a righteous Branch, and a King shall reign and prosper, and shall execute justice and righteousness in the earth (Jeremiah 23:5).

The subjects of this judgment are the *individuals* from the Gentile nations. The Greek word translated "nations" in Matthew 25:32 is *ethne,* and usually depicts Gentiles in contrast to the Jews (see Romans 11:13; Galatians 2:12).

Many of the Gentiles living on earth in the endtimes will already have been judged during the tribulation. The outpouring of God's wrath through war, starvation, and disease will have sealed the doom of many. As we have seen, the Russian hordes will already have met their day of reckoning on the mountains of Palestine. Yet the unfinished business of God's dealing with the Gentiles who lived through the terrors of the tribulation must be taken care of. It is their judgment, to be enacted on an individual basis, that is being described in Matthew 25.

The Gentiles will be gathered together and divided into two classes, sheep and goats. The "sheep" will be at Christ's right hand. They will be allowed to enjoy the blessing of God, and will be allowed to enter the millennial kingdom (vv. 34-40). The goats, at Christ's left, will be cursed. They will be sent to everlasting fire (vv. 41-43, 46).

At first glance, the criteria for the judgment of the Gentiles appear to be their works. Those who manifested the attitude of Christ by feeding the hungry, clothing the naked, and showing generous hospitality to strangers will be blessed of God and share in the kingdom. Those who did not will be cursed.

But a little thought will show that the real basis for judgment will not be works, but faith. According to the Bible, no one is ever saved by works (Ephesians 2:8,9; Titus 3:5), nor will they ever be. Yet the Scriptures often speak of good works as a sign of righteousness, as the natural outflowing of a redeemed life (James 2:26). Today it is possible to show some of the signs of righteousness without being born again. We all know kind-hearted, generous men and women who are not Christians. But this will be impossible in the tribulation. Antichrist will mark his followers with a sign in their foreheads. He'll very likely demand that all Christians be singled out as his enemies. He'll probably hate their lifestyle and be suspicious of all who display it. No, it won't be easy to look like a Christian without being one during Antichrist's heyday. Only those who are genuinely born again will dare to follow the principles of a godly life.

At the judgment of the nations, all who have trusted in Jesus Christ and are born again will be allowed to enter the millennial kingdom. Everyone else will be sent to "everlasting fire." There they will await the final resurrection of the damned, when they will appear before the great white throne and be banished to eternal perdition.

The "times of the Gentiles" will thus be ended. The earth will have been purged. The unjust will have been removed, and the world will be inhabited only by believers at the beginning of the millennial kingdom. The nations will acknowledge Christ's lordship, and will pay Him the homage that is His due. The righteous and just conditions, which God had ordained the nations to establish on earth, will finally have come.

CLOSING THOUGHTS ABOUT RUSSIA

Throughout the long centuries, the common people of Russia have suffered under cruel and oppressive conditions. Few if any of the czars were benevolent and tolerant. For the most part they reigned as iron-fisted dictators, ruthlessly crushing any sign of independence or revolt. The peasants, often a people of deep faith, were little more than slaves to the soil.

Things didn't improve when revolution finally came; in fact, the Bolsheviks turned out to be even more oppressive than the czars. Millions of Russians died in widesweeping purges. The Jews, never safe under the czars, endured an even more fearful existence under Stalin and Khrushchev. Because communism is atheistic, churches have been suppressed, their pastors often imprisoned, and their people harassed. A handful of power-mad men rule by fear this nation of 258.9 million. The people are trodden down under a godless tyranny. Few nations, it seems, have ever fallen so far short of God's original intentions.

Right now it looks as if nothing can stop the Russian bear from accomplishing her goal of world domination. Her rise to power has been phenomenal. Her influence in the world is widespread. Her sights are set on the Middle East, as indicated by her repeated intervention in recent years. At first

Israel's friend, she soon turned against the Jews. She has armed Israel's enemies and supported them in military action.

But Russia's allies in the Middle East have repeatedly failed her. One day a strong Russian leader's patience will wear thin. Seeing his advantage, he'll move his armies southward into the cradle of ancient civilization. He'll make his camp in the holy hills of Judea. But Israel need not fear, for God has promised to protect them. He'll unleash the fury of His judgment upon the invaders, and the troops of the northern federation will fall. The Lord will receive great glory, especially among the Jews. And the wheels of time will have finally rolled around to those terrible days mentioned in prophecy—the great tribulation.

A PERSONAL WORD

My friend, we could be standing on the very threshold of the endtimes. The events we've been describing could occur any moment. Russia is armed and strong. Israel is in the land. A peace treaty with Egypt has already been signed. The nations that will compose the revived Roman Empire could line up overnight. What else awaits? Very little.

Are you ready for the end of the age? Have you received Jesus Christ as your personal Savior? If not, I urge you to do so now—before it's too late. Acknowledge your sin. Admit that you cannot save yourself. Then place your trust in Jesus Christ. Believing that He is the Son of God and that He died for your sins, ask Him to save you. When you do, you'll be free from your sin and guilt, and you'll be accepted into God's family. The events of the final days we've been describing will not affect you, for you'll escape those dreaded days that lie ahead for this wicked world. As a child of God, you'll be in Glory, where you'll spend eternity with Jesus Christ. The Bible says,

> But as many as received Him, to them gave He power to become the children of God, even to them that believe on His name (John 1:12).
>
> He that believeth on the Son hath everlasting life; and he that believeth not the Son shall not see life, but the wrath of God abideth on him (John 3:36).

BIBLIOGRAPHY

Books

De Haan, M. R., *Signs of the Times,* Zondervan, Grand Rapids, 1951.

De Haan, Richard W., *Israel and the Nations in Prophecy,* Zondervan, Grand Rapids, 1968.

De Koster, Lester, *Vocabulary of Communism,* Eerdmans, Grand Rapids, 1964.

Feinberg, Charles, *The Prophecy of Ezekiel,* Moody Press, Chicago, 1969.

Ironside, H.A., *Ezekiel,* Loizeaux Brothers, New Jersey, 1949.

Lee, Francis Degel, *Communist Eschatology,* Craig Press, New Jersey, 1974.

McCall, Thomas, and Zola Levitt, *The Coming Russian Invasion of Israel,* Moody Press, Chicago, 1974.

Spector, Ivor, *Introduction to Russian History and Culture,* Van Norstrad Press, New Jersey, 1961 (3rd edition).

Strauss, Lehman, *The End of This Present World,* Zondervan, Grand Rapids, 1967.

Walvoord, John F., *Daniel: the Key to Prophetic Revelation,* Zondervan, Grand Rapids, 1971.

Walvoord, John F., *The Nations in Prophecy,* Zondervan, Grand Rapids, 1967.

Walvoord, John F., *The Revelation of Jesus Christ,* Moody Press, Chicago, 1966.

Wood, Leon J., *A Commentary on Daniel,* Zondervan, Grand Rapids, 1973.

Wood, Leon J., *A Survey of Israel's History,* Zondervan, Grand Rapids, 1970.

Magazines

Leyasmeyer, Karlis, "Challenge of the Communist," *Bryan Life*, Spring 1979, pp. 8-10.

Mills, David, and Theodore Malloch, "Promethean Faith," *Reformed Journal*, February 1979, pp. 14,15.